Professional Development, Reflection and Enquiry

Professional Development, Reflection and Enquiry

Christine Forde, Margery McMahon,
Alastair D. McPhee, Fiona Patrick

Los Angeles | London | New Delhi
Singapore | Washington DC

SAGE Publications Ltd
1 Oliver's Yard
55 City Road
London EC1Y 1SP

SAGE Publications Inc.
2455 Teller Road
Thousand Oaks, California 91320

SAGE Publications India Pvt Ltd
B 1/I 1 Mohan Cooperative Industrial Area
Mathura Road
New Delhi 110 044

SAGE Publications Asia-Pacific Pte Ltd
3 Church Street
#10-04 Samsung Hub
Singapore 049483

Library of Congress Control Number: 2005937768

A catalogue record for this book is available from the British Library

ISBN   978-1-4129-1936-4
ISBN   978-1-4129-1937-1 (pbk)

Typeset by Pantek Arts Ltd, Maidstone, Kent
Printed in Great Britain by CPI Group (UK) Ltd, Croydon, CR0 4YY
Printed on paper from sustainable resources

Contents

About the authors

Dr Christine Forde is a senior lecturer in the Department of Educational Studies at Glasgow University. She has been involved in the area of professional development for a number of years in the field of leadership and management and particularly working on the Scottish Qualification for Headship. She is the co-author of a book looking at the process of professional development within the field of leadership: *Performance Management in Education* (2002) as well as a number of articles. Her other research interests include gender in education and education, and utopian thought.

Dr Margery McMahon is a lecturer in the Department of Educational Studies at the University of Glasgow. She is Programme Director of the MEd Professional Development and Enquiry – the Chartered Teacher Programme. She is the author of several papers focusing on professional development for experienced classroom practitioners. Her research interests include professional development and identity, and policy process and implantation.

Dr Alastair McPhee is also a senior lecturer in the Department of Educational Studies at the University of Glasgow. He has mainly been concerned with initial and continuing teacher development, and has worked extensively in the fields of access to teacher education, the development of teachers of Music and teacher professional development. He has been the author of a number of papers in academic journals in these areas. He has particularly been engaged with Glasgow City Council in a successful project to widen the applicant pool to teacher education.

Dr Fiona Patrick is a lecturer in the Department of Educational Studies at the University of Glasgow. She teaches on a variety of courses in initial teacher education and undergraduate education. Her main research interest is in teacher professionalism, but she has a background in the history of education, which informs her other interests (the early development of educational psychology; the growth of educational provision in Britain and Europe).

Introduction

This text is designed to provide teachers with a critique of teacher professionalism. It deals with key issues associated with the current debate on professionalism in teaching and what constitutes teacher professional identity. In doing this it recognizes a number of different perspectives: teacher professional formation, research, organizational contexts, learning, continuing professional development and teacher identity. It is important that these perspectives are considered, in a world where 'official' and governmental pronouncements are often more strident than the voices of teachers themselves.

There is another dimension to this book, in that it looks at the English and Scottish education systems and tries to recognize that, in post-devolution contexts, the systemic needs and sociocultural considerations of the educational structures of these systems are different. We also draw upon sources located in Wales and Northern Ireland in our attempt to obtain a more rounded view of what is happening in sometimes very different contexts.

The position from which we start is this: a process of de-professionalization has occurred within the UK education systems over the recent past. Teachers have lost much of their autonomy and agency. This process, we argue, has been introduced with the intention of achieving standardization, benchmarking and performance management. These may have some credibility from the perspectives of systems operation, political imperative and the demands of the standards agenda. But the results have been, in our view, a lessening of the abilities of teachers to control their own destinies and to retain ownership of their own profession. While the rhetoric has been of enhancement of the profession and its image, the effects have been somewhat different.

■ Overview of the Book

Chapter 1 examines the key questions of professionalism and identity, which shape the whole book. It then considers why teachers need to forge new identities in the current climate, examining ways in which teachers shape their identities in different contexts. The concept of teacher professionalism itself and the problems associated with it are then examined in terms of the impact the problems may have on professional identity. Chapter 1 also makes comparisons with other countries outside the UK and with other professions, especially nursing.

Chapter 2 continues the exploration of teacher professionalism, and the way in which the concept is interpreted by different agencies and communities, including that of government. In a world of ever-increasing complexity, the extent to which teachers can be in control of their own profession has altered, and the chapter looks at the nature of this challenge. It considers whether teaching is unique in this respect, or whether a similar situation can be observed in other countries and professions.

Chapter 3 is research based and investigates teachers' views concerning their professional identity. It relates this to aspects such as professional community, self-image and emotion. These are developed and in turn related to confidence levels, well-being and a commitment to professional practice. The chapter concludes that strong senses of self-efficacy and professional identity are vital in meeting the challenges of the changing nature of the profession.

Chapter 4 discusses the concept of the 'discourse of derision' (Ball, 1990) and how this discourse has affected teachers who have to work within the constraints it imposes. The notion of 'crisis' in education in the UK is explored within the argument that the crisis is neither new nor unique to the systems of the UK, but that it has had an effect on how education and teachers are represented to the public.

Chapter 5 examines a concept which has become embedded in the discourse concerning teacher formation and development: that of 'reflection'. The chapter argues that while personal reflection is a very useful tool for personal learning, the impact it actually has on change is limited, and much more sophisticated models of reflection are required if change is to be effective. The Scottish Qualification for Headship is used as an exemplar for this. The chapter looks at the idea that a culture of reflective practice places responsibility for change on the individual teacher, rather than examining the teacher within the context of the policy and institutional environments within which she has to work.

Chapter 6 focuses on organizational contexts within which professionalism and identity are developed. The environments which impinge on the teacher's work are examined, and the tensions which exist between the right of teachers to exercise their professional learning and judgements and the demands of the policies and structures of the organizations within which they operate are discussed.

Chapter 7 deals with the changing role of the teacher within the developing context of the school. This context is defined, in turn, within a range of policy contexts in the UK. The impact of inclusive education and diversity, the development of citizenship, the potential of e-learning and the nature of the learning process are discussed. The chapter ends with a review of the concept of leadership and the location of classroom assistants and paraprofessionals within the school context, and what these mean for teacher professionalism.

Chapter 8 deals with the changes which have recently evolved in terms of the career pathways available for teachers, especially those who are experienced professionals. The development of the 'expert teacher' concept is of particular relevance in this context. The different ways in which this concept has evolved in the varying educational systems of the UK may shed light upon differing models, and the pathways which have been developed have differing purposes and policies underpinning them. The chapter offers a critique of how these pathways are having an impact as they pass through the initial phase of their development.

Chapter 9 extends the critique offered in the previous chapter by interrogating ways in which continuing professional development (CPD) can help to enhance professionalism and redefine identity. Policy initiatives relating to new CPD pathways in the varying UK systems are examined and the relationships between these and teacher identity are discussed. The chapter looks specifically at how teacher identity is enhanced by these initiatives or how they represent a barrier to teachers reclaiming ownership of their profession.

Chapter 10 is the conclusion and deals with the key aspects of professional development, reflection and enquiry. We argue that these are essential if teachers are to fulfil their roles in a meaningful manner in educational and societal environments which are constantly changing. We propose a model of the 'engaged teacher-educator' which seeks to challenge and to extend existing models. We argue that through this model of development, reflection and enquiry, teachers will be able to prepare young people to be learners in an increasingly complex world, and to lead schools and learning in more effective ways.

This text is intended to be of use to several communities of readership. Firstly, it will be valuable to teachers engaging in various levels of continuing professional development, but particularly to those involved in courses or programmes leading to the status of Advanced Skills Teacher (AST),

Excellent Teacher (ET) or Chartered Teacher (CT) where it engages with core concepts. Secondly, the text may be of use to teachers taking professional doctorates, where it will complement other reading which encourages professional learning and development of professional practice. Thirdly, the book may be used by those returning to teaching after a career break and who wish to understand and interpret vital changes within the teaching profession in recent years. Fourthly, the text offers material of use to students in the final year of their undergraduate studies in education, where they will wish to consider the implications of professional formation and entry into the profession itself. It will also offer an opportunity for students taking courses in complementary disciplines such as sociology to consider the relationships between that discipline and education. Fifthly, education managers may find the text useful in providing an analysis of professionalism where the management of teachers and schools is concerned. Those with aspirations for Head Teacher status and who are undertaking courses for that purpose will find it useful in this context. Finally, there are opportunities for work in comparative professionalism.

List of abbreviations

AST	Advanced Skills Teacher
BEd	Bachelor of Education
CLT	Chartered London Teacher
CPD	continuing professional development
CSE	Certificate of Secondary Education
CT	Chartered Teacher
DfES	Department for Education and Skills
ET	Excellent Teacher
ETS	Excellent Teacher Scheme
GCSE	General Certificate of Secondary Education
GTCE	General Teaching Council for England
GTCNI	General Teaching Council for Northern Ireland
GTCS	General Teaching Council for Scotland
HEI	higher education institution
ICT	information and communications technology
INSET	in-service training
ITE	initial teacher education
LEA	local education authority
NI	Northern Ireland
NMC	Nursing and Midwifery Council
NPQH	National Professional Qualification for Headship
NQT	Newly Qualified Teacher
O level	ordinary level
OECD	Organisation for Economic Co-operation and Development
OFSTED	Office for Standards in Education (England and Wales)
PGCE	Postgraduate Certificate in Education
PGDE	Professional Graduate Diploma in Education
PISA	Programme for International Student Assessment
PPA	planning, preparation and assessment

PRD	personal development review
SCT	Standard for Chartered Teacher
SMT	senior management team
SQH	Scottish Qualification for Headship
TACT	Teachers' Agreement Communications Team
TDA	Training and Development Agency for Schools
TEI	teacher education institution
TES	*Times Educational Supplement*
TIMSS	Trends in Mathematics and Science Study
TSW	Transforming the School Workforce
TTA	Teacher Training Agency
USDofE	United States Department of Education

SECTION A

TEACHER PROFESSIONALISM

Reclaiming teacher identity

Chapter outline

This chapter considers the key question of professionalism and identity which shapes the book: *can teachers forge new professional identities which will help them to claim or reclaim ownership of their profession?* It looks at what identity means and how teachers realize their identites in different contexts. The chapter moves on to examine the problems of teacher professionalism as a concept and the impact of these problems on professional identity. International comparisons are made and the chapter also looks at other professional models of identity, especially in nursing.

Keywords

■ Professional identity

■ Professional development

■ Agency

■ Communities of practice

■ Introduction

In this book we argue that teachers need to forge new professional identities in order to reclaim ownership of their profession. We suggest that the way to achieve this is through professional development, reflection and enquiry. The forging of new identities is a critical process within approaches to professional development where it is important to enable teachers to reflect on, and to create, new practices which best serve the learning needs of the children and young people with whom they work. These new practices should centre on an increased sense of teacher agency and ownership of the profession. Arguably, ownership has become vested in other interests. Government policies (in both England and Scotland) retain the rhetoric of professionalism, but nevertheless have served to constrain teachers' professional agency.

Our use of the term 'professional identity' begs the question of what we actually mean by it. We discuss professional identity in this chapter, and will return to this important concept throughout the book to explore it fully and to link it to the issue of practice. For the moment, we want to argue that the complex world of learning and teaching in the twenty-first century requires a professional identity based upon new understandings of what it is to be a teacher.

Classroom teaching now places very different demands upon individuals than it did 20 years ago: these include collegiate working, liaison with outside agencies, new structures and increasing use of new technologies. What is needed is a professional who can respond to rapid change and, when necessary, drive that change. To accomplish this, teachers need to be secure in their understanding of their place within the profession and their teaching identity, and the place of the profession in policy-making. But more than this, teachers are important people. The job they do is central to the lives of children and adults, and in order to regain a full sense of this importance they need to feel that they have ownership of the work they do. This book, in examining the process of professional development, centres around one crucial question, and some of the issues which arise from consideration of it: *can teachers forge new professional identities which will help them to claim or to reclaim ownership of their profession?*

This question is relevant partly because teachers are currently required to comply with an ever more intrusive set of controls: over the curriculum, teaching methods, management, requirements for standards to be met in terms of professional behaviour, performativity measures, predetermined outcomes and targets. Teachers need to contribute to, as well as take forward, policy into practice if they are to enhance achievement. In our opinion, teachers need to reclaim their professionalism, otherwise their professional identities may be established and determined by forces other than themselves. This dislocation of identity can result in a distancing between those who generate policy and those who implement it.

Education policy is currently based upon concepts of productivity and performance, and this is eroding the position and capabilities of teachers to make judgements about pupil learning. As a result:

1 Many aspects of decision-making have been removed from classroom teachers. Decision-making is vital to a sense of professional autonomy. To remove it is to risk leaving teachers with a decreased sense of their own professionalism.
2 Those who feel their professional expertise is under attack may become disengaged with the work they do. Disengagement creates malaise within the profession and therefore within the classroom.
3 Policy specifies an ideal of practice which is too narrow, and which tends to inhibit collegiate working, and which may leave classroom teachers feeling isolated in the work they do.

Underlying managerialist policies lies a construction of teacher identity and practice based upon compliance and conformity that tends to constrain teachers in the formation of their professional identity and in their role as educators. Ultimately managerialism tends to deny individual professional autonomy and agency.

The concepts of autonomy and agency are crucial if we are to consider a process of continuing professional development that genuinely engages teachers in reflecting meaningfully on their practice. It is our intention to return to these concepts at various points in the book to investigate them in detail. We put forward a rounded construction of professionalism which recognizes the importance of individual agency with responsibility to the various groups with whom teachers work, and with respect to policy which teachers are expected to implement. It is for this reason that we prefer to talk about agency as well as autonomy.

We now examine the concept of professional identity to form the basis of our later discussions in which we look at how reflection and enquiry might be used to develop professional identity, particularly in respect of balancing autonomous practice with policy implementation. This is an important issue for this book. Education in the UK in the twenty-first century is largely policy driven: school improvement and pupil attainment are regarded politically as being effected by policy directives. We will argue that improving the quality of the education offered to children depends on more than an outcomes-focused and standards-based agenda. It depends on teachers and how they develop their roles. It is important to spend some time on teacher professional identity at this stage because

> [i]ssues of teacher identity are deep rooted and can be seen to influence the way teachers respond to professional developments, be it with other teachers, the school setting or the pupils themselves. This challenges the process of affecting change through policy development and suggests the need for in-depth professional development that acknowledges the role and impact of teacher identity. (Jones, 2004: 167)

Policy can only go so far in improving educational provision, especially if it ignores questions of how we encourage teachers to develop fully their own roles both at the stage of initial training and during continuing professional development.

■ What do we mean by professional identity?

In putting forward the concept of a professional identity based on agency, we recognize that identity, agency and autonomy can be constructed and understood in very different ways in different contexts. How these things are seen often depends upon positions of power and the relationships within them: professional and clients, school managers and teacher trade unions, and employers. There are issues that we need to consider, not merely in terms of individual practitioners, but in terms of the abilities of an institution to act with degrees of self-determination. Teachers have to work within inherent tensions to construct their own identities.

Teacher identity is not necessarily synonymous with the role and function of being a teacher (see Beynon et al., 2001). Roles and functions are assigned as part of the job and may be outside the individual's control. In contrast, professional identity is constructed by the individual who carries out the role and is based on that person's values, beliefs, attitudes, feelings and understandings (see Beynon et al., 2001: 135). It is also based on our own personal history, ethnicity and culture. Professional identity, then, rests on personal identity but these are not simplistic unitary concepts. Identity is partly individualistic: it is what makes us different to others. However, we also note similarities with others in any given group. Kroger (1986: 6) states that the 'means by which we differentiate ourselves from other people in our lives … constitutes the very core of our experiences and personal identity'. Of equal importance are the similarities which allow us to identify ourselves as part of a group, especially a professional group.

So, our identity has social aspects. Reicher (2004: 929) notes that when we 'behave in terms of any given social identity, [we] are guided by the norms, values, and beliefs that define the relevant identity'. Within a profession we recognize others by their adherence to the norms and values of that profession. Those who do not adhere to these rules risk being termed 'unprofessional', or risk marginalization. Coldron and Smith (1999: 712) state that from 'the beginning of, but also during, their careers, teachers are engaged in creating themselves as teachers … it is a matter of acquiring an identity that is socially legitimated'. During initial teacher education, learning to teach is partly about constructing a professional identity that we are comfortable with, but one which also allows us to feel and be recognized as part of a professional community.

Professional initiation and identity formation

Initiation into the teaching profession occurs first through training/education. Indeed, insisting on a qualified workforce was part of the transformation of teaching into a 'profession'. Philip Gardner undertook a historical study as to how teacher professional identity was formed in early twentieth-century England (Gardner, 1995). This study centred around a time when teacher training was moving from schools to training institutions and where the professional image of the teacher was changing as a result. An interesting aspect of this study is that Gardner uses the voices of the teachers themselves to reflect upon their identities and how these were formed. Many of these teachers undertook the transition from untrained to trained while working in schools.

The retired teachers in Gardner's study indicate that by the middle of the twentieth century to be uncertificated was to 'carry a mask of professional inferiority' (1995: 199). But the interviewees felt that there was a difference in approach to the teaching role: those who were college trained tended to see that as being all the professional education they needed. The uncertificated teacher, on the other hand, tended to see professional learning as something undertaken throughout a career (1995: 199). What college induction did was to consolidate professional identity both at an individual and group level.

The use of examinations and qualifications to 'professionalize' work began on a large scale in the UK in the nineteenth century. Engineers, doctors, accountants, architects, lawyers, all saw their work professionalized by use of formal examinations and curricula to legitimate a certain body of knowledge and skills that their professions deemed necessary for 'expert' practice (see Sutherland, 2001). Partly this was about shaping the values and behaviours that professionals were expected to show: 'formal examinations were seen as the antithesis of corruption and self-interest … [and] ability was equated with merit, talent and virtue' (Sutherland, 2001: 55). Thus a specific image of the professional was created within these groups: one who is knowledgeable, virtuous and expert. It has therefore long been recognized that professional identity can be shaped in part by the education that is designed to induct people into a profession.

Identity formation and career progression

Professional identity, then, begins to be shaped during training/education, but it is open to development throughout a teacher's career, often in response to workplace changes. Woods and Jeffrey's study (2002) examines the way in which primary teachers have had to reconstruct their identities as the education system itself has altered. They mention the sense of consistency in professional identity that was a feature of the 1960s and 1970s. They look at the effects on teacher identity of the challenges to child-centred education, perceptions of a loss of trust (or a change in the nature of trust – see Avis, 2003) and changes in the role of the teacher. Woods and Jeffrey conclude that teachers have seen their role reduced to a list of competences and performativities. In trying to make sense of their professional role, teachers may be forced to assume multiple identities to meet competing demands and expectations, and this can lead to a sense of volatility and uncertainty (Woods and Jeffrey, 2002: 105).

Another aspect of a teacher's sense of identity is expert knowledge. Beijaard et al. (2000) investigated this in a sample of secondary school teachers in the Netherlands. They looked at subject-matter expertise, didactical expertise and pedagogical expertise – the teacher not only as expert in terms of what was taught, but also in terms of how it was taught and how the learners were understood. Most of the teachers saw themselves in terms of a combination of these identities, although it was interesting that many perceived a transition from subject expertise towards learning expertise as their careers developed.

Similarly, Volkmann and Anderson (1998) discuss the development of identity in relation to chemistry teaching. Their conclusion is that the formation of teacher identity is a complex issue, which involves not only the identity of the teacher as a scientist, but also issues of conflict, dilemma and mentoring. One observation from the study is of particular relevance: 'Policymakers who impose top-down change never understand the disrespect they exhibit to the veteran teacher's professional identity' (1998: 308). This suggests that experienced teachers who have practised before the reforms of the 1980s and 1990s may well have developed a different, more stable, professional identity and that this has been challenged in the creation of a new, more 'flexible' teaching force.

■ Contexts for identity: the professional community

In professional life, we work within what Etienne Wenger has called 'communities of practice' (Wenger, 1998). These communities have multiple functions, including functions of learning, collaboration and negotiation. These functions contribute to the formation of identity as participant and learner, because they develop within a range of contexts such as the historical, the cultural, the institutional, and so on. Sachs (2003: 133) comments that communities of practice can have 'profound impacts on teachers' lives both in terms of their classroom practice and in terms of how they construct their professional identities which are exercised both inside and outside of schools'. Thus teacher professional identity is partly formed by belonging to a group or community that is described as 'teachers'. This belonging may well influence behaviour, thinking, values and attitudes.

Professional identity is also affected by the legacy of tradition that surrounds the professional community. Coldron and Smith (1999) suggest that there are a number of 'traditions' which shape how we think about the work of teachers: the craft, the moral, the artistic and the scientific. Consciously or otherwise, teachers use these traditions to underpin the models of practice they use to respond 'to issues and questions arising from practice' (Coldron and Smith, 1999: 713).

The craft tradition represents the idea that teachers use a set of skills and possess a set of abilities which they learn from shared experience in formal and informal ways. This links with the discourse of teacher training in England and Wales – and to the set of professional skills and abilities which are demanded in Scotland. The moral tradition demands that teachers make professional moral judgements, and that they develop their professional identities to align with an ethical view of their work. The artistic tradition relates to feelings, inspiration and the creative impetus. Finally, the scientific tradition sees teaching as being based on an empirical understanding of learning and of the contested notion of 'good practice' (which can then be copied and replicated to solve perceived problems and deficiencies). All these 'traditions' are inhabited by professionals at different times and in different ways, and highlight the complexity of the teacher's role and the way in which professional identity is formed. Though these traditions have changed over time, they continue to coexist and influence understandings of what it means to be a teacher, both in the professional and in the public view.

Other factors can influence identity within professional communities. Sachs (2001) identifies two 'competing discourses' which are instrumental in forming teacher professional identity: the managerial and the democratic. As Ball succinctly puts it, discourses are 'about what can be said and thought, but also about who can speak, when, where and with what authority' (in Jones, 2004: 160). Managerialist discourses highlight accountability and effectiveness and are enforced by authority. Professionalism and professional identity are defined in terms of compliance with these aspects. In contrast, democratic discourses place an 'emphasis on collaborative, cooperative action between teachers and other educational stakeholders' (Sachs, 2001: 153). Sachs goes on to advocate the activist identity, where teachers themselves have control within communities of practice. She argues that teachers' professional identities are 'rich and complex, because they are produced in a rich and complex set of relations of practice. This richness and complexity needs to be nurtured and developed in conditions where there is respect, mutuality and communication' (2001: 160).

New understandings of identity present us with more complex ways of representing the role of the teacher. Figure 1.1 represents some of the complexities involved.

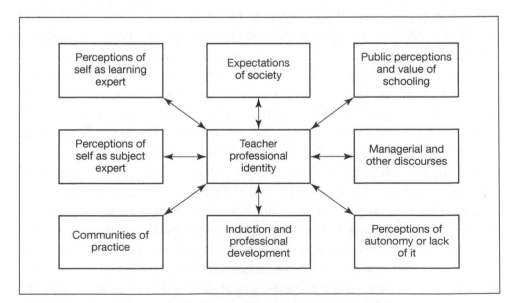

Figure 1.1 ■ Teacher professional identity – important interactions

We have to recognize that personal and social factors are vital to the forging of professional identity. We cannot ignore the role of factors such as gender, ethnicity, culture and social background. In addition, we should acknowledge that teachers' location in the education service is crucial to their notion of professional identity: whether they 'belong' to the early years sector, primary, secondary or special education. Nias (1989), for example, argues for the specificity of primary teachers' professional identity as distinct from other teacher groups. However, things may be moving beyond this idea of specificity – in policy, in initial teacher education, in continuing professional development and in schools there is a greater emphasis on generic issues in teaching and learning which moves beyond the boundaries of job title.

Identity across professions

The complexities inherent in defining identity are evident in many professions, particularly those which have recently sought professional status. Nurses, like teachers, have to form their professional identities within stressful working environments, and have to deal with management and policy emphases on standards, performance and outcomes. In addition, the development of nursing into a degree-based profession has challenged nurses to reconceptualize their roles within complex and changing medical contexts. The onslaught of these changing contexts has led Stronach et al. (2002) to speak of teacher and nurse identities as being 'in flux'. They contend that teachers and nurses are 'located in a complicated nexus between policy, ideology and practice' (2002: 109). Therefore, professional identity is negotiated within situations where identity is affected by dilemmas and difficulties that are often outside the control of the individual.

While there is no agreed definition of what it is, and what it means, to be *a teacher* or *a nurse*, there are broadly accepted personal, professional and academic elements. However, for each individual, personal satisfaction and professional identity may not rest on specific constructs. Ohlen and Segesten (1998) found that professional identity in nurses was strongly related to other personal identities – to, for example, gender identities and self-esteem. There was a difference between those who thought of themselves as *working as a nurse* and those who thought of themselves as *being a nurse* – what Gregg and Magilvy (2001: 53) call the process of 'bonding into nursing'. In other words, a defining moment in our recognition of professional identity may be the moment we *feel* like a nurse or a teacher. Professional identity is therefore a highly personalized construct and one which rests, in part, on our feelings and attitudes about the job we do.

Managerialist institutions like schools and hospitals can too easily ignore the affective components associated with professional identity, for example, self-esteem, self-belief, professional self-confidence. Job satisfaction and motivation are based on such affective elements. This is particularly the case in jobs which require a strong element of personal involvement or commitment to others, such as teaching and nursing. In addition, levels of self-esteem can be affected long before qualified status is gained. In a study of student nurses in Ireland, Begley and White (2003: 398) found that reported levels of self-esteem rose among students as their nursing course progressed, but that by the end of the course levels of self-esteem only reached *average* levels. Indeed, other studies actually show decreased levels of self-esteem among student nurses as they approach registration and qualification (Begley and White, 2003: 398). For example, Randle's study (2003) shows that student nurses' self-esteem 'decreased dramatically' over the duration of their studies (Randle, 2003: 51). She suggests that only when nurses' self-esteem rises within a profession that is publicly valued 'will nurses be in a position to effectively shape healthcare' (2003: 60).

Given the importance of higher levels of self-esteem to coping with workplace stress (Begley and White, 2003: 391) it would seem that to begin your career with self-esteem issues may not augur well for personal well-being and professional satisfaction. In addition, Andersson (1993) found that nurses brought with them perceptions of what it was like to be a nurse on entry to the profession, and that these perceptions remained with a majority throughout their training period, as they hung on to a traditional nurse identity and image. Similarly, much has been said about the importance of reflection in nursing and teaching (see Maich et al., 2000). The evidence suggests that there are similar processes at work in terms of nursing and teaching where identity and integration into the profession are concerned, although care needs to be taken in noting the different contexts and activities of these professions.

■ Conclusion

We have looked at key issues in the definition of professional identity. Discourses of teacher identity have changed: from the individual identity within the collective framework of the early twentieth century, to the managerially imposed identity of the early twenty-first. In the past, professional identity has been shaped by a number of factors:

1 *The expectations of society.* This includes aspects of status and expectation. There was a simpler view of what a teacher *was*, and what was involved in being a teacher. Although the folklore image of the dominie (parish school teacher) possessing high status and respect within communities has endured to some extent, this view has been challenged in recent years. Humes (1986) argues that, even in the past, there were variations in the status and qualifications of teachers which meant that the concept of teacher-as-professional could not be universally applied.

2 *Internal identity based on personal identity.* It is possible that reflective activity was not so evident in the past, and that as a result of this, there was less stress on constantly reviewing and changing identity and performance. Professional identity may, then, have had more stability as a construct for individual teachers.

3 *Notions of learning and the role of the school.* In a society where the pace of change was less rapid, it was possible to hold on to particular conceptions of how learning occurred and how teaching should be carried out. This meant that there was a more widely shared view of learning and the curriculum, and teachers tended to agree this view because it was the 'correct' way of seeing the world (see Paterson, 2003).

Our contention is that teachers need to reclaim the agenda for two critical reasons. First, we believe that teachers have been removed from the decision-making process: that the sharing of good practice has become synonymous with standardization and central control. This has created an apparent crisis within the profession (Avis, 2003) compounded by the fact that responsibility and accountability have been passed further down the chain of command, with the real decision-making being retained at the top. Secondly, we believe that disengagement creates a malaise within the profession and, therefore, within the principal site of learning – the classroom. We believe this does not best serve the interests of learners, teachers and communities. In subsequent chapters we will explore the impact of a culture of performativity on teaching and learning within the classroom.

Issues of change and improvement are at the core of government policy and public priority within education. The standpoint of this book is this: if we are to bring about change and improvement that is meaningful and which positively affects children's learning, then it must be done in a way that places teacher professionalism, and the professional community, at the centre. We also need to realize that, in any change process, teachers may well have to reconstruct their sense of themselves *as teachers*, something that can bring tension as well as opportunity.

2 Teacher professionalism: challenges and tensions

Chapter outline

In this chapter, we explore teacher professionalism. The understanding of this term has changed as it has been subject to different interpretations by different communities, including governments, and by the changing needs of a complex world. The extent to which individual teachers have control over their own profession has changed as a consequence of this, and we investigate this change and the challenges it presents. We also consider whether these challenges are unique to teachers in the UK, and indeed whether they are also found in other professions.

Keywords

 Autonomy

■ Agency

■ Ownership

■ Performativity

■ Managerialism

■ Introduction

Classroom teaching now places very different demands upon individuals than it did even 20 years ago. These demands include working with increased numbers of support staff in the classroom, liaison with a number of outside agencies, new structures (including community and full-service schools), increasing use of new technologies in learning and teaching, varied and differing patterns of community life, and shifting political perspectives on what education can and cannot do. Professionals must, then, be able to respond to rapid change and this is recognized, for example, in Scotland with the McCrone Report (Committee of Inquiry, 2000).

To respond to the many complex demands placed on them, teachers need to be secure in their understanding of their place in the profession and in society. But what are some of the wider issues for teachers in developing their professionalism? We have explored professional identity but now need to turn to the issue of professionalism itself. The next sections consider some of the issues in determining what professionalism might be with regard to teaching. To be considered professional implies certain personal and work-related characteristics: autonomy, commitment, 'ownership' of the work, self-direction. But to what extent are these ideals developed and enabled within initial teacher training, continuing professional development or, indeed, within policy and practice? In order to answer this, we need to look first at what it means to be a professional as distinct from other forms of work.

■ What does it mean to be professional?

In recent years, there was a fairly well understood community of practitioners who were described by the term 'professional' and this community was defined by certain characteristics. For example, practitioners were educated to a particular standard, and were often in possession of knowledge or skills which were not then available to the wider community (see Humes, 1986: 20).

So why is this relevant to teachers? As the concept of the traditional teacher has been challenged, writing and thinking about the concept of teacher professionalism, what constitutes it and how it is realized, have burgeoned. To illustrate this, Avis (1994) sees the concept being used to counter Conservative educational policy in the 1980s and 1990s. He argues that the old, conformist model of the subject specialist is of little use against the direction that educational policy took towards standards and managerialism. A new model, based upon reflective practice was therefore proposed (Avis, 1994).

It is perhaps the notion of autonomy – or the lack of it – which, more than any other, has contributed to present unease with the standards agenda. Autonomy suggests the right to negotiate, and to negotiate from a position of strength. Undoubtedly, this would be the preferred position of the teacher unions. However, the need for teachers to conform to ever more tightly regulated orders and guidelines concerning their areas of professional expertise and knowledge, have compromised this. For example, the need to meet imposed curricular specifications can be seen as one crucial area where the professional freedom of the teacher is seriously constrained. In terms of teacher education and training, a good professional is one who can deliver the National Curriculum within the specified parameters of expertise – not one who challenges these parameters themselves.

■ The importance of autonomy to professionalism

What, then, does autonomy mean for the teacher? We consider autonomy as it relates to subject and pedagogic knowledge and ethical understanding. First, we need to distinguish between autonomy and agency. Agency refers to our individual capacity to influence events, whether personal or professional. It is based on feelings of self-efficacy, that is, the extent to which we believe that we have the capacity to achieve what we think of as desirable outcomes (see Soodak and Podell, 1996). Bandura (2000: 75) argues that self-efficacy plays an important role in human behaviour because it affects our ability to

- set and achieve goals
- think strategically
- think optimistically or pessimistically
- persevere in the face of challenge
- be resilient when faced with adversity and stress.

In addition, it is important to remember that personal agency often relies upon social contexts. Teachers are independent to some extent, but work within the social context of the school. Within the concept of agency it is important to recognize the place for teachers' own creativity and judgement in best meeting the learning needs of children, but this needs to be balanced with societal expectations and institutional accountability. No professional today can hope to be completely autonomous, and many recognize the responsibilities and forms of accountability that go with their work. However, autonomy has traditionally been seen as a central component of professionalism.

Traditional and modern views of teacher autonomy

Traditionally, teacher autonomy has been related to the possession of subject and pedagogic knowledge. It was assumed that at the end of their training/education primary and secondary teachers would have an extensive bank of knowledge about the subjects they teach and about how they teach the curriculum. Professional autonomy and decision-making rested on a foundation of knowledge about how to do our job, and a secure understanding of the subjects we teach. In many respects, if teachers are to claim agency over their work, the claim must still rest to some extent on subject and pedagogic expertise.

However, there are implications here for the way in which teacher training conceives of the place of knowledge and expertise. Both primary and secondary teaching demand extensive pedagogical knowledge and understanding of child learning and development. But when this translates into prescriptive knowledge concerning the delivery of a prepared curriculum, the nature of pedagogical understanding is limited.

In addition, England and Wales has seen the introduction by the Teacher Training Agency (TTA) now the Training and Development Agency for Schools (TDA), of skills tests for entry to postgraduate teacher training courses. If graduate status implies an enhanced level of education possessed by an individual, then the imposition of skills tests in literacy, numeracy and information and communications technology (ICT) suggests that there is a deep distrust of the higher education system among those responsible for the formation of education policy. It also suggests that the tests themselves have been designed to indicate to a sceptical public that action is being taken to maintain standards, possibly in the face of a public perception of 'dumbing down' of standards within universities.

Thus, in terms of teachers' subject and pedagogical knowledge, professional autonomy is curtailed from the inception of a teacher's career. Postgraduate teacher formation is also severely limited by time. There is only so much which can be accomplished in a one-year course – and yet that year is vital in terms of a teacher's professional development. Autonomy is also limited by the prescription of competencies and standards, and by the policy need to manage the system for public accountability. Some forms of accountability are valuable. The question is, what forms? And what role does accountability play in the delivery of education? When standards, outcomes and blunt forms of accountability are given priority over the individual development of the teacher, professional autonomy may be compromised.

The role of the professional body

However, in advocating greater professional agency there is a need to be aware that certain values underpin the idea of a professional. These values tend to be ethical or moral. Humes (1986) draws attention to the importance of an altruistic vision of social service, operated within a framework of ethically regulated working. Other commentators (see McPhee et al., 2003) have noted the absence of an ethical code until recently. The existence of a code of ethical working is generally accepted as an important aspect of professional life and work. There are such codes developed, for example, in medicine. In comparatively recent times, attempts have been made to develop these in teaching, through the Teaching Councils of both England and Scotland. Part of being a professional, then, is to work with recognized and agreed codes and to agree to having the profession regulated by its professional body.

Of course, teaching is not the only profession to be regulated. Nursing has its own ethical code (NMC, 2004). Like UK codes for teachers, it deals with the establishment of expectations of performance. It deals in a similar manner with what is and is not acceptable conduct for members of the profession. However, the code for nurses is much more detailed than that for teachers (either in England and Wales or in Scotland), and gives advice on what is to be done in different situations and dealing with broader ethical issues, including relations with the community. The expectations of professional conduct are clearly delineated and the practitioner – and other system users – are left in no doubt as to what nurses should and should not do. The code concludes by inviting practitioners and members of the public to contact the Nursing and Midwifery Council (NMC) for advice and states that the code is under review at any time (and indeed the August 2004 version is a revision of an earlier edition). The conclusion here is that nurses appear to be more tightly regulated in their ethical code than teachers are, and this may relate in turn to differing perceptions of their professional development.

Both nursing and teaching can present difficult situations in which it is helpful to have a code to guide practice. Nurses, like teachers, face ethical dilemmas, and both professions are characterized by specific moral discourses and practices. In nursing, Pask stresses the importance to professional identity and practice of personal behaviour bound up with notions of 'moral agency': empathy, compassion, understanding (Pask, 2003: 170–1). But many nurses indicate that their training does not adequately prepare them to solve ethical problems (Woods, 2005: 5). Husu notes a similar situation with regard to teachers who often feel poorly prepared for dealing with ethical dilemmas and who are not always aware of the impact of their actions and decisions (Husu, 2003: 311). Therefore, 'a great deal of teaching depends on the teachers' personal presence and their perceptions of what to do in various contingent situations' (2003: 313–14). While personal responses are vital, it is equally important that a profession has an agreed ethical code.

General Teaching Council for Scotland

The General Teaching Council for Scotland (GTCS) is a comparatively mature organization, having been instituted in 1965. It was put in place to exercise supervision of entry and probation for the profession in Scotland and to operate as a structural and disciplinary body for the profession. The

Council is no longer directed entirely by the profession, but has been 'reformed' and 'modernized' to represent a number of stakeholders, not necessarily members of the profession. It can, and does, act on behalf of the Scottish Executive in advising Scottish Ministers about standards and issues such as teacher supply. The danger is that within this situation, the GTCS could be seen to be more concerned with the implementation of policy and standards than with internal regulation of the profession.

This leads us to ask what the purpose of professional bodies might be. If we take the GTCS as an example, it was set up to ensure that societal expectations of, and trust in, the profession and individual teachers could be assured by the profession itself. But the role of the GTCS in defining standards and accrediting programmes tends to move it towards a more directive position in the ongoing development of teachers within a specified policy environment.

We might well question why it has been thought necessary to delegate to the GTCS additional regulation of the profession. The issue is the extension of powers into CPD – it has always had these for initial teacher education (ITE) – and the potential tension between one regulatory function dealing with entry, continued registration and conduct, and the approval of programmes for CPD. On the one hand, one could argue that this places development squarely in the hands of the teachers' own regulatory body and that this is in itself an empowering and professionalizing measure. But, on the other hand, a more suspicious view might be that such a move is part of a wider agenda which sees control as a necessary part of the 'modernization' platform described above.

General Teaching Council for England

In England and Wales, the General Teaching Council for England (GTCE) is a comparatively recent organization, having been established in 1998 as a result of the provisions of the Teaching and Higher Education Act.[1] It has two main functions: first, to act as a regulatory body in terms of standards within the profession and, secondly, to advise the government on education policy *reflecting the views of the profession.*

There are important differences between the bodies: registration is compulsory with the GTCS in Scotland, but not yet so with the GTCE in England. And the GTCE has established a code of conduct and practice for the teachers who are registered with it (GTCE, 2004a). This code specifies similar arrangements in the case of offence to those specified by the GTCS (GTCS, 2001; 2003a), but the code for England and Wales goes further and defines serious professional misconduct in terms of the failure of a teacher to maintain the standard of performance consistent with qualified teacher status (GTCE 2004a: 5).

There are two ways of looking at this situation. One is to say that the teaching profession has to be trusted to behave ethically, and a recognition of its innate professionalism is to see a code of ethical conduct as unnecessary. The other is to state that on behalf of the public, a regulatory body has to lay down a minimum standard of performance which is acceptable, and to define that standard in terms of the criteria laid down for acceptance into the profession. It can also be seen as a reflection of the contested nature of teacher professionalism in the UK: that there is not a consistent vision between the two systems of how teacher ethics might be established and managed. To what extent has the profession itself been responsible for the management and publication of these statements of expectations of performance – and to what extent has it been necessary to design these externally? Serious issues of public perception of the worth of the profession are evident here.

■ Who owns the teaching profession?

Ideally the answer to this question would be the teachers themselves. Teacher agency in professional matters could well be seen as both desirable and necessary, and this agency should extend to an ownership both perceived and actual. However, this is a much contested area and one that has repercussions for professional identity and development. It is our view that government forces have become ever more intrusive into the teacher's world, to the point where teacher professionalism has become seriously affected.

Overall there has been a policy shift towards performativity. Performativity is a concept that dates to the work of Lyotard, who uses the term to refer to processes which are put in place to manage the 'performance-efficiency' of a system (see Cowan, 1996: 249). This emphasis on performativity and on trying to increase efficiency in education in terms of its delivery and 'outputs' has had repercussions for the way in which teachers are allowed to work. Arguably, it has resulted in a move away from professional agency towards surveillance and mistrust of the professional's role.

Furlong (2005: 120) points out that before 1976 teacher professionalism rested upon a concept of autonomy justified by teachers' expertise. This autonomy extended to curriculum development, pedagogic choice and, to some extent, methods of assessment. In the past 30 years, successive governments have moved from the concept of the autonomous professional towards greater regulation, with a particular stress on standards and account-ability. Woods and Jeffrey (2002: 97) argue that, in terms of government policy in the UK, there has been 'an assault on teacher autonomy, and an introduction of far-reaching strongly prescribed changes, sustained over a period, leaving teachers with a feeling of powerlessness. Little attention is paid to their views. They are no longer trusted'.

This movement away from autonomy as a basis for professionalism is not unique to teaching: it can also be observed in nursing and social work. However, it can be argued that the movement has had more impact in teaching than in other professions. Downie notes that

> [w]hereas it is plausible that the legal profession might pronounce from on high and advise the government on technical aspects of government policy as they are affected by the current operation of the law, and it is (almost) plausible that the medical profession can speak with authority on matters of health, it is less plausible that teachers can expect to pronounce on matters of education without being involved in controversy. (Downie, 1990: 158)

Although this was written some time ago, it has become clear that the process to which Downie refers, has become entrenched. Let us consider the areas where teachers have to comply with a set of controls of one form or another.

Curriculum control, professional autonomy and ownership

The government has strengthened its control of the teaching profession through a particular set of mechanisms. For example, in England and Wales, the National Curriculum is statutory. In Scotland, the 5–14 curriculum guide-lines follow a similar path of outlining curriculum content and expectations, though they do not carry the force of law as the basis for external inspections. But in both education systems we see a distancing of the role of the teacher in terms of the writing and preparation of all aspects of curriculum content. 'Ownership' of what is taught has shifted from teachers to government.

There has also been increasing government control in the area of assess-ment. Following a New Right education and accountability agenda in England and Wales, a national programme of testing has been in place fol-lowing the provisions of the Education Reform Act of 1988. National testing has also been a feature in Scotland: however, there was greater initial resist-ance to the idea from parents and teachers (although this seems to have diminished). The nature of the testing process has also changed and there is now a national bank of materials from which teachers may choose in order to confirm their professional judgements on pupil attainment in mathematics and language. Again, teacher judgement over the content and timing of assessment, as well as the use to which assessment is put, has been curtailed.

Arguably the issue is one of who manages teaching and learning. Obviously, teachers still have some ownership of this area. However, government control extends into issues of pedagogy and learning. Furlong notes that there is now 'a huge enthusiasm on the part of the Blair Government to intervene in the detail of educational processes with advice on all aspects of teaching and the day to day running of schools' (2005: 125). For example, on the Department for Education and Skills (DfES) website, there are extensive examples of lesson plans in all curricular areas. This is a clear indication that this government sees intervention in how children are taught and how they learn as perfectly legitimate (although these plans could also be seen as a useful support and resource for teachers). However, one has to ask why such an extensive resource is considered necessary for educated, autonomous professionals. The answer to this lies in the way government infuences teacher training to try to influence the way in which teachers teach.

Training the 'good' professional

Initial training or education is critical to the framing of future professional identity, how teachers see themselves and how they are viewed by society. How courses of training are constructed reflects particular models and perceptions of what the role of the teacher should be. One view which currently carries some weight is that the 'good professional' is someone who delivers government educational strategies, without having a great deal of influence in the formation of those strategies (see Alexander, 2004).

England and Wales

In England and Wales this concept is reflected in the insistence on teacher *training* rather than a more broadly based concept of teacher education. During their training, all trainees have to meet certain minimum standards (TTA, 2003) and it clear that this is designed to meet the needs of the National Curriculum.

It is at this beginning stage of development that important perceptions, values and attitudes are formed, and it is at this stage that government control begins. Of course, not all teachers 'buy into' the standards agenda, and not all teachers have their professional identity shaped in the way that training processes might intend. But the important point is that teacher formation and subsequent development has been seen by UK governments since 1979 as a mechanism to exercise control of professional practice. Furlong (2005: 130) argues that

> individual professional formation is seen as far less critical than it was, especially at the level of initial training. In the lives of young teachers, the state now provides far greater guidance than ever before in the definition of effective teaching, learning and assessment in both primary and secondary schools. And at more senior levels, opportunities for extended professional development are increasingly focused on and achieved through the school as an institution.

The professional community of practice is thus subverted by policy into a community of training.

For example, an important career aspiration for many classroom practitioners might be the attainment of Advanced Skills status. For those who wish to follow a career in the classroom, rather than in the management of schools, Advanced Skills Teacher status is intended to provide an opportunity for professional development and advancement in learning and teaching, including the opportunity to develop the skills of others. In many ways this can be seen as the attainment of expert practitioner status. Once again, however, the standards to attain that status are centrally imposed and controlled outwith the profession itself. The role of the teaching profession in the inception of the standards has been largely advisory. Further, the limited engagement of teachers in terms of take-up[2] with such opportunities for advanced professional development raises further questions about how they perceive their development needs in relation to their professional identities.

In terms of autonomy of practice and individual agency, limitations extend into school leadership. School leaders experience significant constraints on their agency because of the need for accountability and policy implementation. Therefore, questions are raised about the preparation and ongoing professional development of serving head teachers. Are development programmes constructed to drive uncritical policy implementation or to enable leaders to develop school communities of practice to enhance pupil attainment? On this issue we cannot ignore the fact that control and regulation extends into school management,[3] as do specific models of training to gain the National Professional Qualification for Headship (NPQH). At the summit of a teacher's professional development, as well as at the commencement of it, control, management, accountability and performativity are embedded. Johnson and Castelli note that candidates have their training needs objectively assessed in terms of an externally determined set of criteria. In so doing the NPQH is part of a strategy that has already been evidenced in other areas of educational practice such as the National Curriculum, in which a generic model is designed by governmental agencies. (Johnson and Castelli, 1999: 521)

Within the managerialist culture, these are regarded as positive progressions rather than negative ones.

Scotland

In Scotland, the advent of governmental control is just as evident. Initial teacher education is circumscribed by a series of benchmarks, based on a discrete set of competences (QUAAHE, 2000). Courses offered in institutions of initial teacher education must produce students who attain these standards, or they will not be accredited by the General Teaching Council for Scotland, which has general oversight of the accreditation process. Following the Standards in Scotland's Schools Act of 2000, the GTCS has moved into the regulation of the continuing professional development of teachers, including school managers. Programmes leading to Chartered Teacher status and, for aspiring head teachers, the Scottish Qualification for Headship (SQH) must be subject to formal scrutiny and approval.

So who owns the teaching profession at the present time? It is evident that the government, through its various agencies and networks, has an enormous influence over what happens in the educational systems of the UK and over the professional development of teachers. Teachers are subject to controls in curriculum, assessment, teaching methodology, management, professional behaviour and life, performativity and accountability measures, predetermined outcomes and targets. Inevitably these controls have an impact on how teachers frame their professional identities.

The problems of who owns and who should own the teaching profession highlights some of the difficulties in trying to define what it is to be a professional teacher today. Roles have changed, and we would not argue that teaching should stay the same. It needs to develop as a profession. But we must recognize that there are problems in identifying what a profession is, just as there are problems in identifying what it means to be a professional. If teachers are to regain ownership of the profession, what is it they are to own?

■ Professionalism in context: the impact of performativity

In the UK at the present time, performativity manages professionalism. The current culture of performativity and managerialism has been seen by some commentators as both embedded and dangerous. One aspect of professionalism should be a trust that the professional will do his/her job well. But, as Avis (2003) comments, trust in professionals is waning. There is a well-established literature which relates to public perceptions of the teaching profession and to the impact of managerialist policies and policy-making. Ball (1990) is an important thinker in this respect, in that he pointed out the effects of the 'discourse of derision' on the educational community during the years of the New Right influence on Conservative policy in education.

The 'discourse of derision' relates to the perception that teachers and the teaching profession are unable to deliver the required standards of schooling, and that it has been necessary to impose externally derived standards upon them in order to achieve the required goals of society. Thus, it is argued, there is a public perception that the unregulated teaching profession is one of low status and low standards. Ball writes that '[t]he act of teaching and the subjectivity of the teacher are both profoundly changed within the new management panopticism (of quality and experience) and the new forms of entrepreneurial control (through marketing and competition)' (2003: 219).

The results of this sustained discourse have been that morale has been perceived to be low. Bottery (2003), commenting upon leadership in educational communities, argues that what has been created is a low trust 'culture of unhappiness' in which we laud that which can be measured and ignore what cannot be measured, even though it might be as important in the educative process. Wright and Bottery (1997), examining perceptions of professionalism among those responsible for the mentoring of student teachers in the crucial first phase of their professional lives, found that while there was a very strong emphasis on the practical classroom skills, there was very low priority accorded to the wider professional growth of the trainees, or to their understanding of other parts of the educational process. However, once again we must not assume that all academic analysts are of this view: professionalism, as we have noted, is a highly disputed area at the present time. Humphreys and Hyland (2002) argue, for example, that the concentration on performance can be welcomed, provided that it is not narrowly defined in merely technical terms, because such a concentration allows the teacher to flourish as an artist.

However, there are two sides to any argument. Helsby (1996), in a study of how teachers viewed their own professionalism, found both those who agreed that performativity constrained them and those who thought that the education reforms of the 1990s had actually enhanced their professionalism rather than degrading it. Nevertheless, over the past 20 years –and no matter how it is presented in the rhetoric and discourse of the times – there has been a movement which has resulted in de facto control of the profession and a movement away from previously understood notions of teacher autonomy.

Is performativity a UK phenomenon?

It may be useful to look at how these ideas have surfaced – or not – in other countries and how they might have affected other professions. Such comparisons are helpful because they allow us to understand whether what is going on is part of a global process, or whether it is limited to the UK. They also help us to understand whether teaching is caught up in a wider political movement to manage and to make accountable professions and professional practice, or whether teachers have been in this respect, singled out for particular treatment.

Mahony and Hextall (1998: 18–19) point out that although common currents can be discerned in the nation states of the European Union and beyond, conceptions of teacher professionalism within these states are very different. These differences can be accounted for in terms of different cultural, social and political perspectives. Webb et al. (2004) compare concepts of professionalism among primary school teachers in England and in Finland. This study found that in England professionalism was defined in terms of the standards agenda and based on accountability and inspection. In Finland there was a different set of perspectives centred on teacher empowerment:

> most teachers were very enthusiastic about the task of planning their own curriculum. They experienced enhanced self-worth as their work became at the forefront of valued practice. For them the rhetoric of empowerment became a reality and consequently they appeared to view their professionalism as being enhanced. (Webb et al., 2004: 90)

The Finnish situation serves to illustrate that teacher professionalism need not be predicated upon a centrist view of compliance and control.

Similarly, in America, a group of teachers in Missouri attempted to influence the writing of educational standards, in particular the statements of what a student (pupil) might be expected to attain with respect to various elements of the curriculum (Placier et al., 2002). They attempted to make these more relevant to their daily lives in the classroom and to their own constructivist views of the education process. Their influence was seriously limited by the impact of the policy process, and by politicians who had views influenced by the standards debate and by issues of measurability and accountability. Cochran-Smith (2000) also outlines the global nature of teacher dissatisfaction with accountability and public perception issues. In June 1999, 20,000 teachers in Massachusetts marched to the State House to protest about the publication of test scores, and to voice concern about what they perceived to be 'teacher bashing' in the press (Cochran-Smith, 2000: 13). These studies suggest that, in international terms, debates about performance in education have been characterized by conflict.

■ Conclusion

If we are to examine the nature of professional development we need to bear in mind that professional development, reflection and enquiry depend on teacher identity, and that construction of identity is partly a politicized process. We have been critical of a view of professional development which is concerned with the implementation of policy directives and which allows little space for teachers (individually and collectively) to create and shape the learning process within schools.

We have raised concerns about the emphasis on performativity. It is our contention that the teacher needs to work within a broader role than one which is merely technicist. We wish to see the teacher as one who challenges, questions and enlarges the professional role. In subsequent chapters, we will explore how teachers can move forward through a process of professional development, premised on the centrality of reflection and enquiry, to enhance the learning of children and young people.

Notes

1 The institution of a General Teaching Council for Northern Ireland (GTCNI) in 2004 is the latest addition to the UK family.

2 In England and Wales, national statistics for 2004 indicate that there were 3,380 ASTs from a total qualified regular teaching workforce of 410,010. This represents a take-up of 0.8 per cent for Advanced Skills Teacher status. Comparable figures for Scotland, where Chartered Teachers first qualified in 2004, indicate that there were 78 Chartered Teachers from a qualified workforce of 50,963 representing a take up of 0.2 per cent for CT status (DfES, 2004a; Scottish Executive Education Department 2004).

3 In England and Wales, there is a standard to be reached: Statutory Instrument 2003 No 3111 lays down the qualifications which must be held by head teachers of state schools.

SECTION B

EXERCISES OF PROFESSIONALISM

Forming identity: listening to beginning teachers

Chapter outline

This chapter discusses research on beginning teachers' views about their professional identity. It links the concept of professional identity to the role of emotions and the need to feel valued and part of a professional community. It also discusses the importance of these aspects to teachers' confidence, well-being and commitment to practice. The chapter ends by arguing that by supporting teachers to form a robust sense of professional identity and a strong sense of self-efficacy, we may protect them against some of the challenges that arise within a particularly stressful occupation.

Keywords

■ Professional identity

■ Emotion

■ Self-efficacy

■ Introduction

In discussing professional identity it is important to listen to teachers' personal perspectives. In this chapter we discuss the findings of our study on how student teachers perceive their professional identity, how they think they have developed that identity and how they conduct themselves within their professional role. We have already said that developing a professional identity is crucial to how we think and act as teachers. Work on reflective practice and teacher development should take account of the complex nature of professional identity and the psychological and emotional nature of the construct.

We look, then, at issues of identity, emotion and professional development by listening to the voices of beginning teachers, and to the perspectives of those who educate them.

For this study it was decided to focus on secondary teaching, first, because there has already been significant work done on primary teachers' professionalism (see Forrester, 2000; Menter et al., 1997; Nias, 1989) and, secondly, because there is a need to address this area, especially in Scotland. Questionnaires were issued to a year cohort of beginning (secondary) teachers in one teacher education institution (TEI), and to their lecturers. Interviews were conducted with focus groups of student teachers and with individual lecturers in two TEIs in order to better understand their perspectives on professional development and identity formation. Anonymity has been protected by the use of pseudonyms. Data from professional studies[1] seminars over three years are also included to more fully incorporate students' ideas on the nature of the teacher's role.

■ Teacher development: a personal and emotional journey

Hargreaves (2000) notes that education policy and administration tends to pay little attention to emotions. So, too, does teacher education, particularly in the climate of standards and performance management that characterizes teacher education and development in the early twenty-first century. Hargreaves (2000: 812) states that while teaching and learning might not be entirely emotional processes, 'they are always *irretrievably* emotional in character, in a good way or a bad way, by design or default' (original emphasis). Performance management, an emphasis on competence, and a standards agenda, all tend to assume that teaching is a primarily rational enterprise: the role of emotions in teaching and learning is therefore diluted and the role of the teacher becomes bounded within narrow performance parameters.

However, the ways in which teachers undertake their professional roles goes beyond performance. How they perceive their identity (and the ways in which they respond intellectually and emotionally to their work) has consequences not just for their daily teaching performance, but for decisions about their CPD needs. Beijaard et al. (2000: 750) argue that teachers' perceptions of their professional identity 'affect their efficacy and professional development as well as their ability and willingness to cope with educational change and to implement innovations in their own teaching practice'.

Following from what we have said in Chapter 1, developing a professional identity is partly an emotional process. In addition, emotions and mood are important in terms of overall job satisfaction (see Fisher, 2000). This has repercussions for teachers in terms of their likelihood of staying in the job, and with respect to their motivation and morale. Research indicates widespread concerns across many countries about teacher morale and commitment to remain in teaching given the current socio-political climate (see Day et al., 2005). It is therefore important that we pay attention to the role of broader affective characteristics like emotion and mood in the creation and development of teachers' professional identities, particularly at the stage of initial teacher education, if we are to support teachers to feel a sense of professional self-worth in the face of what can be a challenging form of employment.

Identifying with a professional role

Not all the beginning teachers in our study had developed a coherent professional identity by the end of their Postgraduate Certificate in Education (PGCE) year: nor would we have expected them to. What was of some surprise was the number (28 from 82) who said that they already felt like teachers, and that this feeling of professional identity dated to their earliest classroom experiences. Of course, their initial notions of identity may change with experience, and may deepen in complexity. In contrast, the majority of student respondents expected gradual growth into their teaching role and identity, with this being described more than once as an 'ongoing process'. Many highlighted the importance to their identity of completing probation and gaining full registration, with one student commenting on the need to have freedom from assessment before she/he would feel that they were a teacher in her/his own mind. In Scotland and England, freedom from formal assessment will be gained at the end of the probationary year, during which assessment by principal teachers is formative and ongoing.

Another student commented that she/he felt like 'some versions' of a teacher at the end of the PGCE course, but that she/he would not feel like a 'proper' teacher until the probation year. This, of course, begs the question of what a proper teacher is: all the students were working with their own versions of this construct, and the questionnaire results indicate that the constructs were both variable and, understandably, not fully thought through. Marianne mentioned the importance of the personal aspects of teacher identity, and of how initial constructs of the teacher's role come partly from our experiences of being taught:

> At first when I stood in front of the class, I was very impersonal – I didn't feel that my personality was really coming through. Because probably I came from a totally different background, my memory of teaching was back twenty years ago – I had images of teachers I liked and disliked, and when you stand in front of the class you try and fit the pieces together like a puzzle, but you're not too sure exactly what's in the right place. So, I think you play safe by being impersonal. Then I think in the later placements you actually find your personality as a teacher, I think your personality comes through … I didn't have much of a clue who I was as a teacher at the beginning, I was just trying to go by the rules of what teachers do in the school, and then it's like making a recipe where you add your own ingredients.

The importance of allowing your own personality to show seems to be part of individualizing teacher identity. While the students had some common ideas of what it meant to be a teacher, they also recognized that professional identity varied with individual characteristics and behaviours.

In terms of identifying with their professional role, only five students mentioned the importance of practical aspects such as gaining a salary. Most focused on the need to feel ownership of *their* classroom and the need to identify with *their* pupils. Again, these aspects fall into the affective domain, more so than the psychological or material need of remuneration for work done. On the importance of affective elements, Fraser et al. (1998: 62) note that 'teachers who remain in teaching attach greater value to recognition and approval of supervisors, family and friends. Those leaving assign more importance to salary increases, job challenge and autonomy'.

■ What underpins professional identity?

On the whole, the students noted the shifting and tangible nature of professional identity. Two in particular mentioned the tension between the expectations of their role as students in university, and the expectations of them as student teachers on placement. Others stressed the importance of the nature of the school experience to their professional development (whether they had been given responsibility in the class or not, the levels of teaching skill they had developed, building their classroom contributions to a more sustained level).

The students mentioned specific things as being important to the development of teaching identity:

- individual concepts about the role (concrete aspects such as preparing for and conducting assessments, lesson planning, parents' evenings, but also more amorphous elements such as the psychological importance of gaining full registration, being paid, being recognized as a 'proper' teacher as opposed to 'the student')
- location: identification with one school, ownership of teaching space
- professional relationships with pupils, and parents
- relationships with other staff
- being given responsibility for pupils' learning.

Overwhelmingly they identified being valued, and feeling a sense of belonging to the profession, as being vital to fostering a sense of professional identity. Even those who felt their identity to be only partly formed or emergent could pinpoint aspects that were helping to develop some form of specific identification with their professional role. For example,

- feeling valued
- interacting with 'like-minded' people (on the course, in schools and within family and friends)
- the influence of individual personality
- school ethos
- sense of professional community
- feedback from pupils, teachers, principal teachers and others.

Again, it is the affective components that are striking, particularly the need to feel that they belong to a profession which values them.

Feeling valued: a basic need in role fulfilment

Many respondents in our study highlighted the importance of the school context in making them feel valued or otherwise – in particular, the role of the principal teacher, Head of Department, senior management team (SMT) and teaching colleagues. Feeling valued by colleagues was as important as feeling valued by pupils and parents. To feel fulfilled in a professional role we need to feel that what we do is of importance to others as well as to ourselves. Part of developing a strong sense of self, personal identity and professional identity depends on our emotional well-being, and feeling valued seems to add to that sense of well-being. In addition, feeling valued is one of a range of positive work experiences that can help to reduce perceived feelings of stress. Cotton and Hart (2003: 118) recognize that our experiences of stress may be 'caused more by a low level of positive work experiences and positive emotional states' than by larger-scale stressful events in the workplace.

In terms of the importance of feeling valued, there was a difference between the 28 students in the study who already felt like teachers and the 54 who said that their professional identities were still being formed. Of the 28 who already had strong basic role identification, only two did not feel valued. The other 26 all had a firm sense of feeling valued not just by pupils and colleagues (in school and on the course) but by family, friends and even a sense of being valued by society as a whole.

Of those who had a less secure sense of professional identity, there was a more varied reaction. Many did not feel valued, and for those who did, the feeling of being valued was highly context dependent:

- Most pupils make me feel valued – adults less so – a lot of cynical views on teacher competence and professionalism (not always entirely unwarranted!).
- By school yes. By college [i.e. university], no.
- Not really. I see it as an important profession but the media seems to focus on the negatives.
- Not always. Quite often in schools I feel that I am merely the student and that teachers have to go out of their way to help.
- Valued certainly by the pupils as a whole, certainly *not* by the teaching staff I have worked with.
- Generally, no. Society in general and personal friends do not have the respect for the profession that they should. Ignorantly, people see teachers as getting paid for little hours and days in a year. Department and certain students do value me.

So, certain factors seem to influence the extent to which students feel valued in their professional role: support and recognition from university staff on ITE courses (some doubted the value of the PGCE course in supporting their development), support and recognition from colleagues in school (eight students did not feel valued by teachers in school), the feelings of pupils towards the student's work, comments from friends, family and the wider public, and media perceptions.

Developing professional identity and school culture

With respect to working with teaching colleagues, students' experiences were largely positive. The importance of workplace culture to students' developing professional identity is noted by de Lima (2003). In looking at the development of student teachers in Portugal, he finds that there is a tradition of training teachers to be 'isolated professionals' (de Lima, 2003: 197). Part of the induction into teaching during their training year involves students learning how to fit into schools and departments, and in learning how to negotiate professional interactions (de Lima, 2003: 207). Successful socialization into workplace practices demands high levels of interpersonal skills and this was noted by the students in our study.

In addition, students learn to teach within what Lave and Wenger call communities of practice (see Lave and Wenger, 1991). As they work through their initial teacher education programme, students gradually move towards more complex interactions with pupils and colleagues, and fuller participation within the classroom, department and school communities (Maynard, 2001: 41). Learning to belong within these professional communities 'involves becoming a different kind of person ... it involves the construction of identities' (Maynard, 2001: 41). Developing the skills required to integrate successfully into new communities of practice takes time, but can also demand reappraisal of professional identity.

In our study, the students appreciated certain things in terms of helping them to fit in with, and adjust to, departmental culture. Support and advice were welcomed, but also being given some measure of responsibility – and what might be termed agency – for lesson planning, pupil assessment and styles of lesson delivery. This helped them to feel that they were being treated as teachers to some extent, rather than only as 'students'. From work with students in PGCE seminar sessions, one group identified their understanding of the complex nature of working with colleagues. While they noted few difficulties working with teaching staff on placement, they described a range of strategies they used to 'fit in' with the existing teaching staff: asking advice about teaching and learning, asking advice and information about working with particular pupils, focusing on what was expected of them as students, and staying mindful of their role as students and the expectations that accompany that role.

However, as confidence grows, so does a need for some recognition of being in transition. Some students mentioned the need to be recognized by other staff as being more like a 'teacher' than a 'student' in the later practices. This accords with Woolfolk's research which indicates that teacher preparation programmes 'must support and encourage increasing autonomy ... This means prospective teachers need to assume more and more responsibility for real teaching over the course of their preparation as they gain knowledge and skill' (in Shaughnessy, 2004: 162).

■ Characteristics of professional identity

What characteristics does professional identity have for the students in our study, and why are these characteristics important to the teacher's role? First, the nature of personal and professional characteristics are important to perceived self-efficacy and to positive aspects of teachers' work, such as caring and commitment (see Sutton and Wheatley, 2003). Secondly, these characteristics are important in terms of whether or not individuals are likely to remain in teaching. Chapman and Green (1986: 273) note that there are six factors involved in teacher retention: personal characteristics, educational preparation, initial commitment to teaching, the quality of the first teaching experiences, professional and social integration into the teaching profession, and external influences such as the employment climate.

We asked our students to highlight the professional characteristics they considered to be necessary to the work of teachers. The majority expressed their view in terms of affective and interpersonal components. Only one person mentioned intelligence, and few mentioned core teaching skills. Most focused on aspects such as: commitment to the job, understanding and caring for pupils, respect, compassion, dedication, dependability, personal and professional integrity, and the importance of personal values and belief systems. While it was acknowledged that certain job-specific skills were vital (communication skills, effective classroom management and time management) the stress was firmly on the personal and interpersonal factors that underpin professional identity and role. Also important was a belief that teachers can make a positive difference to pupil learning.

This finding is supported by work done in the professional studies seminars over three years. During seminars, students are asked to identify what they see as characteristics of effective teaching practice and of professional practice (including identity). Both at the start of the PGCE year, and at the end, they place a stress on the importance of interpersonal and affective aspects. In looking at the responses generated by students in three cohorts there was a stress on the following:

■ providing encouragement and motivation for pupils
■ being approachable, but able to encourage limits for pupil behaviour
■ being seen to be caring, and willing to listen to pupils
■ being interested and interesting
■ trying to be open-minded, and not pre-judge pupils
■ trying to be creative
■ diplomacy (with pupils and colleagues).

Many students mentioned, both in class sessions and in the interviews, that they initially had not worked out their professional 'tone' and demeanour: that they had started out on the 'wrong foot' with some classes and some pupils. There was an awareness from several students that professional behaviour can strongly affect pupils and that teacher interactions can promote behaviour in pupils that has a bearing on class ethos as well as on the pupils' attitudes to class work (see also Sutton and Wheatley, 2003: 340). Students in seminars had a strong awareness of the complexity and difficulty of classroom interactions and a realization that skilled interaction with pupils and colleagues takes time to develop.

Autonomy and agency as factors in professional identity

Overall, respondents felt that the amount of autonomy they had depended on certain factors. Apart from government policy, specific in-school factors were mentioned: the role of the principal teacher, senior management team, the school environment and ethos, and the demands of the curriculum. Management styles were found to be either autonomy enhancing or reducing. Fifteen student respondents felt they had been given considerable amounts of autonomy as beginning teachers, with the ability to create and be creative with lesson content and planning. One commented that they had been encouraged to try different teaching approaches and 'depart from the norms'.

There was no expectation of unlimited autonomy, more an expectation of individual agency over some key aspects of their work. However, a significant number (20, that is, 24 per cent) felt that they had not been given enough opportunity to direct what and how they taught. The students perceived that this was either because of the demands of curriculum and assessment, or because class teachers or principal teachers were unwilling to allow students to depart much from specific expectations of how to teach. When asked about the amount of direction and control they had been given on teaching experience, students mentioned the following limiting factors:

- Very little [autonomy]. A packed curriculum which has been fixed. Little scope to deal with the consequences of disruptive behaviour. Insufficient support from management: all minimise autonomy.
- Very little. We service the exams not the students. Perversely, you have more [autonomy] the less ability the students have.
- I feel I have control over my teaching style. However it would be nice to be able to choose what I teach.

- As a trainee, not much, all the schools I've worked in have been prescriptive in what should be taught.
- Government: encouraging competition between schools. How can this be a good thing? Putting pressure on teachers. Focus should be on teaching and learning.
- Compromised by restrictive management styles, or by being obliged to continue dealing with students who you consider it beyond your competence to teach.
- Some teachers want their class taught in a very specific way – quite narrow minded. Some teachers like to check everything you are teaching their class.

On the whole, most students (62) felt they had some degree of autonomy, 48 stated that they felt that their autonomy had been partial, limited they felt by the fact that they were students. However, some felt that they should not have been granted the same degree of autonomy as a fully qualified teacher might expect.

Our study indicates that the amount of agency student teachers have may vary with context as well as with stage of education. Although most were not autonomous in the purest sense of the term, many were allowed a high degree of responsibility in developing lessons and some were actively encouraged towards creativity in lesson planning and delivery. Fraser et al. (1998: 66) found in their research into teachers' job satisfaction, that teachers at the beginning of their career were more satisfied with the amount of autonomy they had than were teachers with longer service. It may well be the case that, as one person responded, unlimited autonomy is undesirable: they felt that what is required is some autonomy within a supportive department and school environment.

Identity, confidence and well-being

To develop teaching confidence, and to form a robust sense of professional identity, we need to build self-efficacy. Woolfolk notes the importance of initial teacher education in fostering this, and argues from her research that '[t]eachers' self-efficacy for teaching – their perceptions about their own capabilities to foster students' learning and engagement – has proved to be an important teacher characteristic often correlated with positive student and teacher outcomes' (Woolfolk, in Shaughnessy, 2004: 154).

In addition, self-efficacy can be viewed 'as a protective factor' against workplace stress 'as it has a direct impact on psychological distress' and its associated symptoms (Chan, 2002: 566). This aspect is particularly important given that teaching is acknowledged to be one of the most stressful occupations, with teachers suffering greater levels of stress than those in comparable professions (see Evers et al., 2002: 228). Feelings of self-efficacy may help protect against burnout, and may also enable teachers to cope with curriculum and pedagogic change more successfully than those with weak or negative feelings of self-efficacy (see Evers et al., 2002: 237).

At interview, students felt that being given a degree of responsibility for teaching and learning was important to their developing confidence and efficacy as teachers as well as to their feelings of agency. Steven (a mature student) commented:

> My first school placement I felt as though I was given a lot of responsibility and I was quite confident in my own teaching … But my second school I felt as though they adopted a policy that there was always someone in the room with you and that the responsibility was taken away from me. I felt as though my teaching was damaged by it … So there was an element I felt, as though you weren't really trusted, which I didn't like.

On the whole, the students thought that the PGCE course had helped them to build their confidence as teachers. Some began the course with no confidence in their potential ability to teach: others began with confidence but found that various aspects of the course negatively affected this.

Ellen related her lost confidence to her first teaching experience:

> I was terrified and I had a really bad teaching experience dealing with discipline in my first week. I wanted to leave and never come back. Two girls just started fighting in the class and I didn't know what to do. I think I was just nervous and I was quite disappointed in myself. I mean, in the other job that I do as a staff nurse I've stood up to a 6'2" guy who wanted to tear my head off my shoulders, but I've never felt as much pressure as I did in that classroom.

The negative emotions associated with uncertainty or feeling out of control in the face of challenging pupil behaviour are well documented (see Sutton and Wheatley, 2003: 333–4). Some students in our study found that having to deal with discipline issues affected their ability to decide how they taught; others found that it affected their confidence, and that responding appropriately to challenging behaviour was seen as one of the more 'daunting' aspects of learning to teach.

Most students (41) felt that the PGCE course had helped them to gain knowledge of teaching and learning, and the majority (51) stated that they had learned significantly from teaching experience. On the other hand, Susan commented that the reflective element of the course had initially lowered her confidence:

> I think [the course] knocked you right back, and then you started to question everything you did – absolutely everything. But then gradually it builds you up more, so that at the end you feel confident that you have the ability behind you: the confidence is justified. That's one responsibility the tutors have got, a huge responsibility, because you start off with nothing and then you build up.

Overall, the professional studies element of the PGCE was seen by most students as having made a positive contribution to their development as teachers. Indeed, one student commented that he is now a 'much happier person. I was dissatisfied with the place I was in before, thought I wanted to do this, wanted to be good at it, and I'm absolutely loving what I do now'.

While the majority felt that teaching experience was ultimately positive, the stress involved, and the steepness of the learning curve, can be considerable:

> I was absolutely shattered by my final placement. Physically, mentally, emotionally – totally drained. The expectation of you in your final placement you think is going to be really high and when you go in you're under so much pressure, plus I had a few issues at the school I was in with another teacher in the department, and I ended up in tears with the regent, and by the end of it I was so glad to leave the school that I was wrecked physically and emotionally. But when you think 'I've survived this, that and the next part' you think you can do anything.

> I think the three placements were difficult physically because you are on the go all the time, and you don't realize … when you're working for other companies you do a 30-hour week and you go home and that's it. And for some reason, when you're working with children you feel physically more tired than when you're working for a business. Even at weekends, you don't totally relax. You're thinking of the next lesson you've got to plan, and you never put anything down – it's, like, right, I need to go and do this tonight.

I've had to work very hard. And that was most difficult in the first placement. I was *tired*! But I've got to watch that I don't get too intense, too focused. I am conscious that I could just be working too much.

I was told on my first placement that I was really good with the one on one, and I was fairly comfortable doing that, but I wasn't really being a teacher. I was told it was as if I was trying to teach them individually rather than as a group. I had to learn to stand there and have a presence. It was very daunting.

Before I started the course, I didn't realize how I'd have to organize things in the minutest detail – I didn't realize before I started that things could get more chaotic than I wanted them to be ... Reflecting on how I saw teachers, I thought it just all happened. Now I realize that it doesn't ...

Teaching is a stressful job, and the ongoing stress can lead to teachers leaving or seeking early retirement (see Friedman, 2003). In addition, high dropout rates in the first years after leaving initial teacher education are of concern – not just in the UK, but in America, the Netherlands and Australia (see Goddard and O'Brien, 2003; Kassem, 2002; Manuel, 2003; Stokking et al., 2003; Weiss 1999). It would seem that disillusionment can set in at an early stage. For example, Goddard and O'Brien's study of beginning teachers indicated perceptions that teaching was a job that involved high workplace pressure where perceived effort was higher than reward (Goddard and O'Brien, 2003: 106).

Figures for England show that dropout rates run at 18 per cent for teachers leaving within three years of training; 30 per cent overall for 'post-training wastage'; and 15.8 per cent for annual retirement (Smithers and Robinson, 2001). Smithers and Robinson (2001: 2) found that reasons given for leaving teaching centred on workload, pupil behaviour and government initiatives.

This is sad because the leavers had often come into teaching with idealism and commitment. Many had positively chosen teaching, sometimes after experience of other employment. They said they were looking for something worthwhile that was not linked to targets and the bottom line. They wanted to work with children, pass on their enthusiasm for their subjects and enjoy the freedom of the classroom. They were leaving because they perceived these satisfactions to have been eroded. (Smithers and Robinson, 2001: 3)

It may be that newly qualified teachers begin with ideals that are not matched in reality (see Friedman, 2003; Stokking et al., 2003; Goddard and O'Brien, 2003). However, the student teachers we interviewed all showed a sense of realism about the work they were about to undertake as teachers: they had experienced the difficulties of teaching, and were under few illusions about the nature of the work. They felt that they had begun to develop skills to enable them to cope with the challenges while recognizing that their development as teachers was just beginning.

Overall, the majority of the students in our study realized that their understanding of what it means to be a teacher, and their knowledge of how to fulfil the complex demands of the role, would take time to develop and that they were at the beginning of the journey to develop their professional skills, knowledge and identity. In looking at the students' perspectives it becomes clear that they had been encouraged to look at their developing identities. But what of the people who teach them? In what ways do the ideas of teacher educators try to encourage identity development among beginning teachers?

■ Encouraging identity development in initial teacher education

Seventeen lecturers in two faculties of education were asked about professional identity and the extent to which their ideas on this underpinned their work with student teachers. The lecturers work on a range of courses: Bachelor of Education (Primary), Bachelor of Technological Education (Secondary), Bachelor of Education in Music (Secondary), PGCE (now PGDE – Professional Graduate Diploma in Education) Primary and Secondary. They also undertake delivery of CPD for experienced teachers.

All but two respondents stated that they worked with an idea of the professional characteristics they would want their students to consider, if not to begin to develop. These characteristics mirrored the PGCE student responses in our study. Most of the professional characteristics mentioned by the lecturers were personal or interpersonal, with only two mentioning subject confidence and up-to-date knowledge, one mentioning organizational skills, and two stating the importance of knowing and using learning theories. However, none referred to specific professional skills such as classroom management, lesson planning and delivery, or collegiate working. The emphasis was strongly on the person who would be teaching rather than on what one respondent referred to as the craft element of the work.

Core personal skills were described as: being committed, reflective, caring, approachable, flexible, self-aware, conscientious, valuing the self and others, trustworthy and having integrity. Being knowledgeable seemed to take more precedence than any narrow concept of intelligence as a desirable professional characteristic. What comes through in the lecturers', and the students', responses is the complexity of personal and interpersonal skills that are required as a foundation for being a successful teacher.

How lecturers conceptualize their work and practice

The lecturers mentioned their part in supporting critical reflection and encouraging students to consider what the teachers' role means for them. One stated: 'We encourage them [the students] to be self-aware, critically reflective and informed. We hope they will question the system and develop a sense of who they are as a teacher, rather than what they *do* as a technician.' Four lecturers mentioned the need to take a wider perspective within teaching, to move from being a technicist towards being a professional who recognizes the social and political issues that surround teaching and which affect pupils in schools. One termed this a 'sociological perspective' which asked students and teachers to look

> not just at their remit but at the society they function within, and at other societies; that is, they are aware of the danger of being ethnocentric at both a micro and a macro level. This could mean they have, at least, the potential to rationally analyse and manage the factors linked to planning, implementing and evaluating 'effective' teaching ...

The need to encourage students to interpret policy, especially curriculum policy, was clear from the responses.

Another lecturer stated that they would wish their students to become the type of teacher who 'is not bound by policy documents, but is able to look at policies and see what the words are saying ... and consider why the policies have arisen and what the underpinning arguments of these policies are'. For this lecturer, it was important that the students analyse policy within the context of understanding 'who their children are', to relate policy analysis to their pupils and to apply their understanding of policy 'to help their children to be creative learners who are in charge of their own learning'.

For some of the respondents, issues of social justice were important, and so it was essential for them that the social and political contexts for learning were discussed with students. Another highlighted the fulfilment that comes from having students understand the reasons why you encourage them to look at broader issues. This lecturer wrote:

> I am in a sense political; I am committed to certain values and visions of society and the place of teachers and education in such a framework … I suppose when forced to think about it, I want my student teachers to share my values and vision and not just be technically competent, but understand and feel emotionally that the teacher is an essential public professional … In a sense I am the message, I must model and meet the standards I set for my students.

Modelling practice was evident throughout the responses, and was seen as one way to introduce and develop discussion on what effective teaching and learning actually is.

For some lecturers, there was a sense of modelling not just the technical aspects of the work, but the core professional and personal values that they felt were most important to teaching.

> It's not just the way I teach students, it's also the way I engage with them in other ways. I try as much as possible to be an example to them and in the same way I would hope that they would be an example to those they educate …

> I try to practise what I preach! If I want them [the students] to be committed and enthusiastic, it helps if I come across that way! I am a very analytical person by nature, and I analyse the people I teach and the strategies I then use to teach them. I try to make the students aware of the importance of this too.

> Values and beliefs shape how any teacher teaches – this can be negative and positive. I try to present a consistent model which demonstrates [professional] skills and values.

Discussing core values as well as issues of social awareness was seen by some of the lecturers as being an important background for students to understand and encourage children's learning. One lecturer wrote that teacher identity is 'intersected' by pupils' experiences and socialization: teachers do not work in isolation – there are cultural and personal factors that affect whether or not teaching is successful, and affects what counts as successful teaching. These cultural and personal factors are complex and vary from school to school, as well as within and between classrooms.

Modelling practice and discussing what ideas underpinned that practice were seen as one way to encourage students to recognize that there is no single correct way to 'teach'. But it was also recognized that teacher educators need to have a concept of their own teaching identity in order to model what they consider to be effective practice, and in order to encourage reflection in their students. Yet, professional identity is as complex for teacher educators as it is for students, even to the extent of asking whether a lecturer is a teacher, or what form of teacher they are.

For some, their own sense of professional identity was not regarded as being fully delineated, but it was present and tended to be evident in their teaching philosophy and the values and ideas which underlay their practice. One lecturer said:

> My beliefs and values about learning and learners provide a philosophy from which I develop approaches to teaching. My interest in learner involvement, equality, and respect for the learner, all inform my choice of teaching style and content. I am open with students about this and encourage them to develop their own philosophy too – based on critical reflection. So I encourage them to look at their work through their own beliefs and put them under scrutiny.

The issue is one of 'engagement', as another respondent mentioned. But there was no sense that any lecturer expected students to work through challenging issues of professionalism and practice to become a confident professional by the end of their course. There was a sense that professional ability takes time to develop and that 'some take longer than others to grow in professionalism and confidence'.

There was also a belief that students need to be supported not just towards professional reflection, but also to develop the 'craft' elements of their work. At times, the more technical aspects would have to take precedence:

> I do think you have to be aware – particularly as the students are progressing on the course – of being a critical friend. I visit them on practice … They can become quite dependent on somebody coming in and telling them 'If you do x, y, and z, you'll be absolutely fine'. You asked about models of reflection before – I think that's something that becomes more sophisticated as you go on. But if you walk into a school, and the situation's absolutely desperate, the student can't see a way through … then the first thing you might have to do is maybe help to dig them out of that, before they're willing to engage in trying to solve the bigger problems for themselves.

Understanding that students can be in difficulties that mean they can no longer reflect meaningfully on their practice is an important aspect in tailoring support for students. So, too, is the realization that not all students can manage to reflect in a sophisticated way at the beginning of their careers. It is all very well to speak of developing agency and reflective ability in students but, as this lecturer states, when students experience a crisis of confidence or loss of ability in practice, there is a need to focus on the immediate goal of helping the student to find coping strategies and to improve in the short term. The longer-term goal of developing reflective awareness may have to wait.

Lecturers' models of practice

Despite mention of the 'reflective teacher' in their responses, lecturers were not tied to definitive models of teaching or teacher development. One said that they resisted a

> narrow view of the teacher and the kind of skills that the teacher should have … I'm quite open to them being very different teachers at the end [of their course]. I think what I'd like them to know is, I'd like them to be reflective and self-aware, and I'd like them to know about what are their strengths and how do they use them best in their teaching. I don't want them to go out and think or be told 'if you're more like the teacher in the next class you'll be more successful' …

The need for students to develop their own ideas and philosophy of teaching was clear. There was a sense for some that, without this, beginning teachers might be drawn towards narrower, more technicist models of teaching. This issue was raised by a respondent who felt that teachers had to understand that behaviourism is not the only model of learning, if it is a model of learning at all, and that students needed to develop awareness of a range of learning theory, and to appreciate that learning 'is socially constructed and culturally oriented'. Another stated that, while students should keep up to date with learning theory, it was important that they use this to 'recognize and develop their *own* style of teaching'.

Another mentioned the wish for their students to develop into teachers who had 'drive and ambition', however they might define that for themselves. They wanted to encourage their students to become 'a teacher who is able, at quite an early stage, to begin to articulate how they see their career panning out. So, taking responsibility and recognizing that a degree in education, or a qualification in education, is actually a fantastic thing to have, and can open lots of doors'. Others mentioned this aspect in less detail, referring to the need for students to be flexible in meeting career challenges, and to be able to work within a job that can be subject to enforced change and variation.

However, there was concern that students had to develop their ideas about teaching and their teaching role within highly pressurized courses. This aspect was spoken of as affecting not just the students but how fully they were able to engage with the students:

> the very tight timetable of the undergraduate and PGDE students while they're here … means that it's quite difficult for me to enable the kind of student that I would like to see who has independence and creativity because they're constantly at classes or out on placements, and that's a very different pattern from other undergraduates.

This highlights the issue of student teachers needing time and space to think and to develop not just as teachers, but also in personal terms:

> I don't think they're getting time to be students. I think they're student teachers – particularly the BEds [Bachelors of Education]. I think in fourth year with the major project we try to let them be students and some of them can't be, some of them don't know how to be, some of them don't know how to have freedom because there's been so little opportunity the rest of the time. That might change, because we are developing within the new degree more student-centred learning, more problem-solving, more peer assessment, more sustainable assessment, and so I think it will change.

So, it may be that the emphasis on developing identity and professionalism within four-year courses could militate against a more holistic view of intellectual and personal development. This tension reflects the earlier comments from some PGCE students of the need to move between different identities: the personal, the 'student' and the 'student teacher'. These students also felt that they moved into a transitional identity towards the end of the PGCE course – an identity that was more closely aligned to expectations of a qualified teacher. Our study indicates that the complex and shifting nature of professional identity for beginning teachers, and for those who teach them, should not be underestimated.

■ Conclusion

In many countries, teaching has been subject to rapid change and diverse sets of expectations in the past 20 years. This change can lead to uncertainty for teachers and to a questioning of their professional role. In Australia, Day et al. (2005: 567) note that

> Policy changes and reformist imperatives have left many teachers feeling confused about their professional identity, the extent to which they are now able to use their discretionary judgement – arguably at the heart of their sense of professionalism – and about their capacity to carry out the responsibilities associated with their new performativity identities which challenge traditional notions of professionalism and professional purposes and practices.

In the face of such challenge, morale and motivation can be affected, as can commitment to a teaching career. If teachers can be supported to develop a robust sense of professional identity, with a recognition that their identities may have to continue to develop with career stage and with differing contexts, then they may be more likely to sustain commitment and to cope with change.

How then, might more experienced teachers be helped to (re)consider their professional identities? We will look at this issue in detail by focusing on the following issues: the policy pressures on teachers in the twenty-first century; how reflective practice might be used to develop identity and enhance professional practice; and how the school and teaching community might develop an atmosphere of collegiality rather than of performativity.

Note

1   In Scotland, the professional studies course is a core element in initial teacher education. It is taken by all students on a course, and provides knowledge and understanding of educational research, theory and classroom practice across a range of key issues.

Teacher professionalism in an era of 'crisis'

Chapter outline

This chapter identifies some of the strands that have made up what is known as the 'discourse of derision'. The main aspects of this discourse are discussed, and the roots of the 'crisis' in education are traced in the UK. The purported crisis in education standards is neither new nor limited to the UK, but it has had a significant effect on how teachers are viewed politically and by the public.

Keywords

■ Discourse of derision

■ Accountability

■ Performance culture

■ Policy agenda

■ Introduction

It is agreed by many commentators on education policy and professionalism that teachers now work within an ethos of performativity, generated and legitimated by government policy. Since the 1980s there has been a strong current in education policy of demanding specific forms of accountability and of tying these to simplistic measures of rising/falling pupil achievement. These issues are seen not just within the UK education systems, but in Australia, the USA, New Zealand, the Netherlands and in many European states. But where has this policy agenda come from, why does it hold such credibility today, and what are some of its effects on teacher professionalism?

This chapter examines the roots of the standards agenda and the promotion of a discourse of underperformance and educational failure. We seek to understand why these discourses are unhelpful, and why policy is failing to take account of what is meaningful in educational terms. In doing this we agree with Avis (2005: 209) that 'the contradictions and limitations of performativity provide the context in which new forms of professionalism can develop'. Teachers cannot simply ignore educational policy, nor can they choose to opt out of school cultures which emphasize performance management and audit culture. However, given the strictures that these things impose on individuals, how can teachers best be supported to develop professionally so that they can gain more agency within their teaching practice and within the school community?

■ The constraints of the performance culture

In the UK, one policy document in particular has set the agenda for New Labour thinking: the 1998 Green Paper *Teachers: Meeting the Challenge of Change*. Although this policy document does not extend to Scotland in terms of legislation, it does illustrate and underpin government thinking, and so may indirectly affect the shape of Scottish policy to some extent (although the policy community in Scotland is distinctive in many respects). In it, the Labour government speaks of the 'imperative for modernisation' of the teaching profession (Chapter 1). This centres on an acceptance of accountability, and a compliance to the demands of policy. The document states (DfEE, 1998: 1:13):

> [modernization] demands a new professionalism among teachers. The time has long gone when isolated, unaccountable professionals made curriculum and pedagogical decisions alone, without reference to the outside world. Teachers in a modern teaching profession need:
>
> ■ to have high expectations of themselves and of all pupils;
> ■ to accept accountability;
> ■ to take personal and collective responsibility for improving their skills and subject knowledge;
> ■ to seek to base decisions on evidence of what works in schools in this country and internationally;
> ■ to work in partnership with other staff in schools;
> ■ to welcome the contribution that parents, business and others outside a school can make to its success; and
> ■ to anticipate change and promote innovation.

The government was in no doubt that *all* schools 'including those in the most disadvantaged circumstances, can take up the challenge of raising standards. We will recognize and provide support for schools facing economic and social disadvantage, but this cannot be allowed to be an excuse for under-perform- ance' (DfEE, 1998: 1:4). And so the agenda was set: policy management not just of the education system, but of the individual teacher's professionalism. Of course, this is not to say that all teachers were or are unthinkingly compliant in accepting government policy, nor is it to deny that there are many teachers who agree with the direction in which government policy has taken us. However, there are concerns about the nature of government policy, its educational rationale, and its construction of teacher professionalism that have been well documented, but which also bear further examination.

Government policy in the UK, and in other countries, tends to rest on uncritical and often unexamined beliefs and truisms about teaching as a pro- fession, and about the nature of teaching and learning. The government's acceptance in its Green Paper that there is a holy grail of 'what works' in terms of improving pupil 'performance' is a testament not only to its narrowly defined outcomes for our schooling systems, but also to its belief that simplis- tic measures can be introduced to drive up standards (for example, the introduction in England of the 'literacy hour'). The belief in simplistic meas- ures, often devoid of underpinning by serious research or exhibiting unawareness of it, has led to the introduction of rafts of education policy directives and to the implementation of a series of measures designed to improve children's literacy, numeracy and overall educational performance, without actually bearing in mind the very complex social and economic con- texts in which children underachieve. As the Green Paper states, educational disadvantage is now 'no excuse' for educational failure – not for schools, teach- ers or pupils. The culture of blame is therefore brought into play: if schools and teachers do not raise standards, they have failed and must accept responsi- bility for that failure rather than pointing to mitigating circumstances.

Such policy ultimately rests on a reduced and limiting idea of teacher professionalism and education policy. The teacher is now part of a wider 'enterprise culture' who works in a world of quality, service, clients, stan- dards, performance and improvement (not just of standards and outcomes, but of themselves) (see McWilliam, 2000). The enterprising school is now expected to excel in examination results, national test results, specific areas of excellence, pupil experience, parental satisfaction, public accountability and in creating business and community links (see McWilliam, 2000: 77).

Moreover, enterprising schools and their teachers are now involved in high stakes: not just in trying to ensure individual pupil performance, but in contributing to the performance of the economy.

In his first term as Prime Minister, Tony Blair spoke of the need for education to support the growth of the 'knowledge-based economy' (Blair, 1999: n.p.). He spoke of the need for us to gain a 'whole new attitude to learning' if 'we are to succeed in the knowledge economy' (Blair, 1999: n.p.). This stress on the education system's contribution to economic performance is not limited to New Labour policy: Day et al. (2005: 564) mention the pressures on Australian teachers to 'ensure that they contribute maximally to the economy of the country in which they work'.

But Blair went further than this type of broad linkage. He directly linked success in the knowledge economy to the performance management of teachers:

> And critical to reform are our teachers. I appeal to them. You do a great job in our schools. We know how important it is for you to work as a team. But if we are to get the real step change in your pay you and we both want, we have to link it to performance. We have to raise standards, and we have to remove those who really cannot do the job. (Blair, 1999: n.p.)

Of course, it is agreed that we want to have school systems in the UK that are excellent, and that we want to have schools which give our children a strong chance of educational success: the question is one of how we support and encourage teachers to do this. Do we accept Tony Blair's vision of performance management and directive policy, or do we look for other ways of encouraging teachers to use their professional expertise to enhance pupils' learning in a broader sense? We look more closely at this last issue in Chapters 6 and 8. For the moment, the issue concerning professional practice is expanded upon.

Policy and the professional teacher

The impact of recent policy initiatives in the UK and elsewhere has done little to encourage a notion of teachers as expert professionals. Indeed, much policy seems to uphold a stereotypical view of teachers as lacking the will to improve and the skills to help pupils succeed. In the USA, policy initiatives which stress teacher accountability measures have been introduced: for example, see the 'No Child Left Behind' Act of 2001. US education policy, like that in the UK, takes a punitive stance on those districts and schools which fail to raise standards, and subjects them to 'corrective action' (see Webb, 2005: 190). 'No Child Left Behind' speaks of 'closing the achievement gap between high- and low-performing children, especially the achievement gaps between minority and nonminority students, and between disadvantaged children and their more advantaged peers' (USDofE, 2001: s. 1001/3). But it speaks of this laudable goal within a clear agenda of performance management and accountability. The Act states that it has as one aim:

> holding schools, local educational agencies, and States accountable for improving the academic achievement of all students, and identifying and turning around low-performing schools that have failed to provide a high-quality education to their students, while providing alternatives to students in such schools to enable the students to receive a high-quality education. (USDofE, 2001: s. 1001/4)

As with UK policy, this begs the question of whether or not accountability measures are there to promote surveillance or collegiality (see Webb, 2005) and of what forms of accountability we wish to use to improve children's education. It also begs the question of whether or not governments are removing themselves from their duty to tackle the socio-economic causes of educational failure. While schools can and do have effects on pupils' educational achievement, wider socio-economic factors cannot be ignored.

In addition, as Bartlett (2004) notes, American teachers are not often accorded public sympathy:

> The mass media and many policy-makers, together with a general folkloric perspective, often depict teaching as a low-demand occupation requiring little time and posing few difficulties. The argument goes something like this: teachers, compared to other Americans, appear to have short work-days, free weekends and long summer holidays. Furthermore, tenure insulates teachers from job insecurity and allows them to keep their jobs regardless of competence, effort or investment. (Bartlett, 2004: 566)

But this view ignores the reality: the expansion of expectations of the teacher's role, the lack of understanding that working time for teachers expands beyond the seemingly short school day without additional pay for 'overtime', high levels of teacher stress and burnout, and worrying numbers of teachers leaving the profession within the first five years after qualification (see Kassem,

2002; Smithers and Robinson, 2001; Stokking et al., 2003). And the countries in which issues of stress, teacher dropout and early retirement are of most concern tend to be those with the strongest performativity policy agendas.

■ Discourses of crisis

The policy imperative upon constant educational change adds to a feeling that education is in crisis and that underperformance is endemic. There is some evidence from comparative analyses (Programme for International Student Assessment – PISA; Trends in Mathematics and Science Study – TIMSS[1]) that test and examination results for pupils in England and Scotland place these countries lower on the list than they would wish to be. However, to extrapolate a situation of crisis from these results is to exaggerate the situation within UK schools. Certainly, not all children meet expected age-related standards in national tests, but this is one of the problems with introducing national tests: some children will inevitably fail them, or do less well than a comparative indication of what they should be able to do at a given age. It is worrying that within the UK some pupils leave secondary school without qualifications, and with difficulties in literacy and numeracy. However, the reasons why this happens are often based on complex individual and familial situations, as well as on social and economic factors.

There are certainly specific difficulties and stresses for teachers and pupils within schools, and it is of concern that a range of school effectiveness research indicates that there are differences in outcomes between schools serving similar communities (Reynolds et al., 2003). It is also of concern that research into teacher effectiveness does not seem to have influenced teaching practice to any widespread extent (Reynolds et al., 2003: 88). But the hard evidence for a crisis in the UK education systems is limited. So why does this discourse persist?

In part, the discourse of crisis is engineered by governments and by their insistence on rapid changes of policy to try to promote short-term rises in narrowly defined standards. Government and education authorities tend now to take a 'carrot and stick' approach to school improvement (Scott and Dinham, 2002) and this approach to improving quality is now widespread. (It is evident in the UK, Australia, the USA and New Zealand, for example.) The discourse of crisis calls attention to the role of teachers, and promotes a culture which stresses 'doubts' about their 'competence, quality and professionalism' (Scott and Dinham, 2002: 16). A school improvement agenda has been set up, with little meaningful debate on what needs to be improved and why. Within this culture, 'calls to change education have frequently been cloaked in the language of improving standards or quality. The unspoken corollary of this is that opponents must be in favour of low standards, poor quality teaching or similar' (Scott and Dinham, 2002: 19). And, so, simplistic battle lines are drawn: either you are with a government in its aim of averting crisis and improving standards, or you are against it.

This emphasis on crisis in education has arisen in part from what has been called the discourse of derision, where the teaching profession is derided and a culture of blame is instigated. This discourse has become a factor in shaping public attitudes to teaching, and in shaping UK government policy to control the teaching profession and to set up an agenda where school improvement is linked to examination performance rather than to a holistic view of what children need from their educational experiences. How then, did this discourse come to have such prominence?

The 'discourse of derision'

The phrase 'the discourse of derision' was used by Stephen Ball (1990) to describe New Right discourses relating to wider areas of activity than education. Ball draws our attention to a number of key historical events and players in the challenges made by the New Right from the 1970s onwards to so-called 'progressive' intellectual thought, and towards the impact which this thinking had on education in particular. Like other commentators such as Denis Lawton (1992), he outlines the development of this New Right current of thought from the Black Papers of the late 1960s which were critical of what has been called progressive methods in education. The media at the time played its part in highlighting such criticism when attention was drawn to the William Tyndale primary school in 1975. The school was charged with using progressive methods which failed to teach children the basics of a sound education.

In fact, the situation was much more complex. Davis (2002) highlights a set of tensions within the school and between the school and the local authority. The context for the tensions is summarized by Davis (2002):

▪ disagreements between teachers in the school over teaching methods (widely seen as tension between the progressive and the traditional teacher)

- local authority deference to teacher autonomy leading to the use of progressive methods at the school
- parental objections to the teaching methods used.

What was a difficult situation characterized by argument between teachers and their managers, and with parents, and with the local authority, was reduced in the media to a statement about the 'failure' of progressive methods within the school (see Davis, 2002: 275). Thus began one strand of a media and public reaction against progressivism, with no clear understanding or analysis of what exactly progressive teaching methods might be.

Further criticism of teachers was apparent in James Callaghan's Ruskin College Speech of 1976: 'Towards a national debate'. In this speech Callaghan, then Prime Minister, highlighted what he considered to be pressing educational issues for the Labour government. He stated: 'I have been very impressed in the schools I have visited by the enthusiasm and dedication of the teaching profession' (Callaghan, 1976: n.p.). However, he continued: 'I am concerned on my journeys to find complaints from industry that new recruits from the schools sometimes do not have the basic tools to do the job that is required' (Callaghan, 1976: n.p.).

He then went on to highlight what he perceived to be a lack of science and mathematics skills among school leavers, and commented on the numbers of girls who dropped science subjects at an early stage at school. He also asked questions about what should be in the core curriculum of schools, what form examinations should best take, and what form post-16 education should take for those 'less-academic' pupils (Callaghan, 1976: n.p.). And he issued a warning:

> To the critics I would say that we must carry the teaching profession with us. They have the expertise and the professional approach. To the teachers I would say that you must satisfy the parents and industry that what you are doing meets their requirements and the needs of our children. For if the public is not convinced then the profession will be laying up trouble for itself in the future. (Callaghan, 1976: n.p.)

Britain in the modern age, with new technologies and new industries would need a skilled workforce. Callaghan was convinced that young people at the time lacked the necessary skills. Bartlett (2002: 529) argues that this speech 'with its implied criticism of the work of teachers and standards in schools, can be said to mark a change in government attitude to the autonomy of the teaching profession'.

Moving towards accountability

The Ruskin College speech of James Callaghan in 1976 paved the way for a new vision of teacher accountability and this has been energetically pursued by both Conservative and Labour governments in the UK. However, we are wary of advocating for a 'return to teacher autonomy' that seemed to exist pre-1976. Essentially this notion of teacher autonomy is both mythic and nostalgic, and represents a deeply conservative construct of harking back to a golden age. Thus, it may be seen as unhelpful in the current debates about what it means to be a teacher. This retrogressive construction of teacher autonomy is akin to a culture of laissez-faire, which might be described as 'closing the classroom door'. In other words, teachers remain isolated from the wider organizational and policy contexts. We have to acknowledge the circumstances that partly led to the significant change in policy direction in the UK in which education – like other public services – was scrutinized for efficiency and teaching – like other professions – was made more accountable in the public domain.

The 1960s had seen major changes in philosophy, in pedagogy, and in the curriculum. These were perhaps most readily identifiable in the primary sector following the publication in Scotland of the Primary Memorandum (Scottish Education Department, 1965) and the Plowden Report (CACE, 1967) *Children and their Primary Schools*. Such changes were also influential in secondary education with the development of Standard Grade in Scotland following the publication of the Munn (SED/CCC, 1977) and Dunning (CRATFYSES, 1977) Reports in 1977, and the introduction of General Certificates of Secondary Education (GCSEs) evolving from ordinary levels (O levels) and Certificate of Secondary Education (CSE) examinations, in England in the early 1970s. This represented moves away from traditional didacticism and formal examinations to a focus on the processes of learning. These reports also represent the days of child-centred education, discovery learning, teacher experimentation and apparent professional freedom.

However, all was not entirely positive. The publication of the report *Born to Fail*, which had been commissioned by the National Children's Bureau, charted the systematic failure of the school system to enable children from disadvantaged backgrounds to achieve their potential (Wedge and Prosser, 1973). Rutter et al. (1979) demonstrated the ways in which some schools could routinely alienate pupils from their role as learners. They also showed that some schools seemed to be able to engage learners more positively in the processes of learning. Rutter et al.'s study also argued that teaching and learning processes could be influenced by school ethos. School-wide influences, particularly leadership, could impact on the range and quality of teaching strategies used by teachers and therefore on the quality of pupil learning experiences. Clearly, this era of autonomy where decisions about the curriculum were left 'to the profession' meant in practice that many teachers were left without any wider frame of reference, aside from public examination systems.

In addition to issues of autonomy, debates over the efficacy of 'modern' teaching methods have been going on in the UK ever since the Ruskin speech. These debates crystallized most notably with the Conservative government's call of 'back to basics' under (Prime Minister) John Major. In his 1993 speech to the Conservative Party, Major called for a return to *traditional* teaching methods (see Wintour and Bates, 1993), again with little explanation of what these are, but in the knowledge that the public would understand: teaching of reading and writing largely based on rote learning, written tests and teacher-led lessons. Such 'New Right' Conservative thinking appropriated public fears over state education without giving strong supporting evidence as to why the so-called progressive methods were being labelled a failure. Lawton argues that one of the principal reasons for the success of New Right educational thinking and its influence on policy throughout the 1980s and early 1990s was the failure of the Labour Party at that time to put forward coherent counter-policies based on an alternative ideology (Lawton, 1992: 30). The adoption of essentially Conservative education policies by the post-1997 Blair governments may well have been due to this ideological vacuum.

Certainly, the discourse of derision found political voice under the Thatcher and Major governments (1979–97). The Conservative years saw an unprecedented level of education acts, and a strengthening of educational direction from the centre. In particular, initial teacher education was 'reformed' because the conservative administration saw teachers as being 'wedded to outmoded, left-wing, collectivist ideologies and to the principle of individual autonomy ... Most important of all, teachers believed in "progressive" educational ideas where knowing "how to teach" was seen as more important than being an expert in "what to teach" ' (Furlong, 2005: 122). Furlong (2005) argues that Conservative governments still saw teachers as central to the education system, but wished to change their role by introducing a new concept of professionalism whereby teachers were now meant to implement government policy about how and what to teach, and how and what aspects of the curriculum to assess. Educational reform continues under Tony Blair's direction: as Ball comments, in the early twenty-first century, the 'scope and complexity of the [education] reform agenda is breath-taking' (Ball, 2003: 217).

■ 'Derision' in the modern era

Two of the more interesting features of the 'discourse of derision' are its longevity and its scope. From the nursery sector to university, the assumption is that teachers should be doing better, and mistrust of educational academics is also apparent, particularly their role in initial teacher education. Chris Woodhead (2002), for example, is very clear that the correct location for the training of teachers is the school, rather than the university: 'The best way to train the teachers of tomorrow is alongside the best teachers of today' (2002: 176). Common sense, is it not? And appealingly simple. As Furlong notes (2005: 128): 'One of the things that has been "flattened" is the complexity involved in professional education: the current, school-based system is now accepted as largely unproblematic.'

Woodhead's solutions to a range of apparent failures in the education system are clear, and carry with them the weight of his former experience as England's Chief Inspector of Schools. He sets out the problems of state schools as he sees them: falling standards, failing schools, disengagement of learners, the lack of opportunity for young people from areas of deprivation. Woodhead's solutions are based around the application of clearly defined educational standards and a clearly defined curriculum, basic approaches to assessment and testing using the results to compare school performance, creation of a market, vouchers and the involvement of the private sector. From a common-sense point of view, it all makes perfect sense.

The problem is, of course, that the difficulties which face our education systems today are not as clear or as simple as Woodhead would have us believe. We are told that standards of academic achievement are falling, that young people cannot perform straightforward tasks which their predecessors could, and that they lack knowledge and understanding of a range of subjects. Against that, we have evidence of increasing numbers of examination passes at all levels in both England and Scotland: in England the rise has been fairly dramatic, in Scotland less so. So what then, are we to believe? Can we simply attribute the examination results phenomenon to grade inflation? Or is it evidence of a genuine rise in standards? And if this is the case, then how do we explain the perceptions of skills and knowledge deficits in our young people?

The situation is a complex one, with many different layers of meaning and possible explanations for observed phenomena. This complexity is recognized by Tooley (2000) who arrives at conclusions which share some common ground with those of Woodhead, but who conducts a more thorough discussion of the issues and debates, and draws on global perspectives in doing so.

Perhaps the real role of the 'discourse of derision' has been to entrench the view that the only way to address the 'failings' of educational provision is to adopt 'common-sense' solutions based on performative measures. The best agency to achieve this is now seen as the government, not the teachers themselves. Beginning with the Thatcher governments in the 1980s, through the Major and Blair eras, the government has promoted the view that *it* is best placed to deal with educational problems since it has a strategic role and therefore is best placed to form the policy initiatives which will put matters right. The result of this thinking is that England now has 'one of the most highly politicised and rigidly controlled education systems in the Western World' (Grainger et al., 2004: 243).

But we have had initiatives and policies to address perceived educational problems for the best part of a quarter of a century, if not longer, and still the rhetoric of deficit continues. For instance, in Scotland, we now have the 'Schools of Ambition' initiative (Scottish Executive, 2005) which is beginning in 20 selected schools. These schools will have freedom from an externally defined curriculum and so will be able to develop specialist areas. In addition, they will receive enhanced funding to develop strong links to their local communities. They must be dedicated to transformational change, and if they do not demonstrate success in raising standards their status will be reappraised. It remains to be seen whether this in itself is the design and implementation of a peculiarly Scottish take on the specialist schools policy which has been a major element in New Labour educational reform in England, or whether it is a genuine attempt to move away from top-down curricular planning to allow schools to develop learning in response to the needs of their local communities. It also remains to be seen whether the reality of the initiative will match the rhetoric.

■ Conclusion

Since the 1970s there has been a sustained 'discourse of derision' which has questioned teachers' professionalism and has accepted, with little measured evidence or debate, that state schools are failing in a number of ways. Hard evidence for this failure is limited, indeed national examination results improve year on year. However, the discourse of derision has led to a lack of trust among many: a lack of trust in the state system and a lack of trust in teachers to educate all children to the best of each child's abilities. Government policy now trusts the power of outcomes: systems of educational testing and accountability are put in place to attempt to force improved standards. The government is no longer fully accountable for the economic and social difficulties faced by many families and their children: teachers must raise educational standards despite the complex legacies of social deprivation. It is easier to mistrust the individual teacher than to mistrust the new system of accountability.

Of course, we should take care not to argue that all in the education garden is rosy, or that there was a halcyon era of teacher autonomy where all children learned and no teacher lacked ability or commitment. The William Tyndale saga highlights the difficulties that can arise when teacher autonomy has no supporting policy or management context. And, without doubt, government and industry still point to areas of skills gap which schools and young people need to try to remedy, while many schools struggle to best educate young people with additional needs within a policy of inclusion.

If there is now a perception in government policy and elsewhere that we cannot waste the potential of any child, and that we must maximize the potential of all if we are to survive in a knowledge economy, then the government must support teachers in their efforts to promote effective teaching and learning in schools. The government has chosen to follow a narrow conception of effective teaching, and to set standards and centralize control of the teaching profession. Having done this, where can such a managerialist approach go in the future, except to increase the policy detail and further centralize control? However, the government could choose a different approach which might encourage teachers and schools towards professional agency, creativity and decision-making, in order to allow the potential of teachers to encourage more effective learning.

It is fair to argue that the discourse of derision has not led to much profitable debate, in politics or in public, about how teachers and schools should best be supported to provide a quality education for children. Standards must rise, and teachers must continually educate themselves to improve throughout their careers. In a sense, teachers are being asked to evaluate themselves continually, and possibly to keep recasting their professional identities. The effects of this career-long improvement will be looked at next: what are the repercussions of lifelong reflective learning for teachers, and what models of learning might be most applicable to giving teachers support to continue to learn, rather than simply being seen to 'improve'?

Note

1   The Organisation for Economic Co-operation and Development (OECD) Programme for International Assessment (OECD, 2003): conducted in three-year cycles. The focus is on the academic performace of 15-year-olds across 40 countries, specifically in the areas of literacy, numeracy and scientific literacy. The Trends in International Mathematics and Science Study provides data which compares the performace of school students in the USA with students from other countries.

5 Professional Reflection: Identity, Agency and Change

Chapter outline

This chapter challenges the notion that professional reflection is necessarily beneficial to practice. While it argues for its usefulness as a learning tool, it cautions that more sophisticated models of reflective practice need to be used to promote practice change. It looks at the development of one such model within the Scottish Qualification for Headship, and argues that the culture of reflective practice tends to place the onus for change on the individual practitioner, rather than on looking at the political, policy and institutional contexts within which change needs to take place.

Keywords

■ Reflective practice

■ Critical reflection

■ Social dynamics

■ Introduction

Reflective practice is now seen as one of the key ways for teachers to develop understanding of their work at all stages of their career. Given the current tendency to question levels of teacher professionalism, and the tendency for policy and standards to stress performativity, models of reflective practice can offer teachers an opportunity to develop their professional identities and teaching practices within what can be a challenging working environment.

e practice is now so widespread across a range of profes-
almost become clichéd. Yet it has the potential to be a
for professional learning and development. However, not
ctive practice are equally valuable, or equally sophisticated,
actice has tended to become subsumed into performance
measures, particularly where it is linked to salary enhancement via CPD. Of
course, care must be taken not to stereotype the role of the teacher as being
either a critical reflective practitioner or a straightforward policy deliverer.
The reality is more complex than that, and teachers' roles will most likely fall
between these two paradigms. Teachers cannot choose simply to ignore government and local authority policy but, in asserting a claim to professional
status, they must deliver this policy in a way that best enhances children's
opportunities for learning.

This chapter explores some of the issues involved in using reflection to
enhance professional practice, but it also looks at some of the difficulties surrounding the concept of reflection, and asks whether or not we need to look
at professional development in a wider context rather than focusing mainly
on the individual teacher.

■ What is reflective practice?

It is intended that using critical reflection will allow teachers to identify what
they do well and what they need to do to improve in their practice. Using
reflective practice is now widespread among many professional groups, both
at the initial training stage and during CPD. It is especially prevalent in
teaching and nursing where it is believed that modern professionals must
think consciously about their practice to move them towards deeper levels of
awareness not just about what they do but about why they do it. As Burrows
writes: 'If professional practice is about change, development and meaningful
conscious action, the art of reflection becomes a pre-requisite' (Burrows, in
Maich et al., 2000: 309).

Open-minded and flexible approaches

Reflecting on practice is therefore meant to enable practitioners to be more
open-minded and adopt more flexible approaches to their work, so that
they are better able to cope with modern working practices which are often
characterized by the need to respond to, and initiate, change. It has therefore
become popular in those professions where change has become a consistent

feature and where it is often imposed: teaching, social work, nursing and general medical practice. With respect to the training of doctors, Mamede and Schmidt state that the 'changing context of health care delivery and the growth of the medical knowledge base are placing high demands on the doctor's expertise. Indeed, clinical practice has become increasingly characterized by change, ambiguity and complexity' (Mamede and Schmidt, 2004: 1302). In any profession that is prey to ambiguity reflective practice is now seen as a means to enable professionals to cope with and respond to imposed change which may leave them struggling to find a definitive purpose for their professional role.

Underlying beliefs and assumptions

In addition, reflective practice is meant to promote analysis of underlying beliefs and assumptions that practitioners might hold without having a full appreciation of why they hold them and what alternative beliefs might have equal credence. Particularly in teaching, our own educational experiences 'create deeply ingrained attitudes and beliefs' that form the personal philosophy which underlies our professional practice (Griffin, 2003: 207). This philosophy can exert a powerful influence to the point that it may override what is presented to us during our professional education (see Griffin, 2003: 208). For example, with beginning teachers (and with some who are more experienced) a common notion is that theory and professional studies tend to be less relevant to them than learning that takes place in schools. The dominant notion is often that

> field experiences – no matter how they are designed – are the best way to acquire professional knowledge and competence as a teacher. This notion can be observed in student teachers' negative attitude towards theory ... and their uncritical way of evaluating any kind of field experience as simply the best learning context in teacher education. (Hascher et al., 2004: 626)

Using reflective practice with students may therefore enable them to see a value to their academic studies that they had not seen before because it challenges them to look consciously at what they take for granted in terms of their underlying attitudes.

Empowerment

At its strongest, the reflective practice movement asks us to go beyond the individual level to critique institutional and government policy and practices. And for writers like Sachs, the goal of reflective practice is not just to change the individual but to empower them to move towards activism and a 'questioning of the status quo' (Larrivee, 2000: 296). It may be that reflective practice has become popular precisely because its focus is on individual change while giving opportunities to critique existing institutional and management practices. Many professionals feel disempowered by managerialism and reflective practice seems to give us a way of focusing on ourselves: if we do not have the power to change the system at least we can critique it, and at least we can try to change our own practices in ways that might resist the worst excesses of the managerialist style. As we shall see, this emphasis on changing the self has both positive and negative repercussions.

Reflective practice: the search for a definitive model

It is easier to say what reflective practice is meant to do than to say what it is. Many models exist, and there is confusion over how to define reflective practice conceptually. Courses and texts that advocate reflective practice suggest a variety of methods: narrative storytelling that allows the practitioner to interrogate their versions of events; reflective journals; critical incident technique; reflective group discussions; problem-based learning and so on. McLaughlin (1999: 10) mentions the lack of a coherent philosophy or practice and the fact that reflective practice rests on such a variety of models that it is difficult to say definitively what it actually is. Models of reflective practice do tend to stress, following Schon and Argyris, the concept of reflection in and on action, and of reflection leading to practice change.

However, it is difficult to give a definitive model of reflective practice. Certainly, those models which advocate reflection can help us to make implicit knowledge about our practice more conscious. They can also help us to examine our unexamined beliefs and attitudes and to understand the impact they have on our practice (see Thurlow Long and Stuart, 2004). However there are doubts about the levels of reflection reached by professionals, especially those who are beginning their professional education. Many find difficulty in moving from descriptions of practice to analysis, particularly with a view to placing their experiences within broader contexts and issues for practice (see Admiraal and Wubbels, 2005).

Gould and Masters (2004: 54) highlight the widespread enthusiasm for reflection but note also the criticism that 'centres on the lack of a common definition, its unproven benefits and the absence of a universally acceptable structure for its implementation'. It may be that seeking a definitive model is not strictly necessary. What may be required is for professionals to work with a model that can be used across a range of disciplines, a model of reflection which recognizes the need for change not only at individual level but within wider institutional and policy contexts. We return to this issue later in the chapter when the Scottish Qualification for Headship is discussed.

Certainly, those models of reflection which are most beneficial tend to be those that are based on encouraging practitioners to critique their practice and the assumptions and values that underlie it (see Day, 2000). It is important, too, that reflection focuses on 'personal, social, institutional and broad policy contexts in which practice takes place, and the implications of these for the improvement of that practice' (Day, 2000: 123). In addition, reflection does allow one means for professionals to 'grapple with and understand the complexities of practice and the uncertainty and confusion that they provoke. Rather than looking to external sources for answers individual practitioners are enjoined to look within themselves through a process of reflection' (Taylor, 2003: 245). However, this very stress on individual solutions to complex issues can mean that the onus for change rests less on the institution in which the professional works, and more on each professional her/himself.

Despite the lack of a definite model, there is evidence to suggest that practitioners do feel that reflection is beneficial to them. It is worth looking at research evidence here to try to ascertain in what ways reflection can help professionals to consider their practice.

■ Reflection and learning

Certainly, many professionals do find it difficult to reflect at a critical level. This is especially the case with beginning teachers and with those who are newly qualified. However, as Harrison et al. (2005) note, with support, critical reflection can be achieved and can be helpful in developing practice and can encourage newly qualified teachers towards a sense of agency. It can also help to make explicit tacit knowledge (Sparrow et al., 2005) and can encourage practitioners to link their existing knowledge to research and theory in their field.

In addition, reflection can help practitioners to see themselves as able to make decisions over their work in terms of defining their own practice (see Pedro, 2005: 50). It is also helpful at the stage of initial teacher education in terms of trying to help students to see teaching as being a complex and dynamic activity rather than as a behaviourist enterprise (Pedro, 2005: 51). Of course, this is not as straightforward as it sounds, because each professional needs to develop her or his own understanding of what reflective practice means for them, and the lack of definitive models does not help her or him in this task. Having said this, student teachers can be helped to become more reflective and critical given appropriate levels of support (see Pedro, 2005).

Individual understanding and beyond

Seeing teaching in a broader, less reductivist sense, is important, as is gaining understanding of the elements of the work that rely on artistry and emotion. Reflection can help us to see that we bring a range of personal as well as professional skills to our work. Johansson and Kroksmark (2004: 358) mention the benefits of reflection in helping us to recognize and develop 'intuitive pedagogical action' which might otherwise go unnoticed or be downplayed. There seems to be a wealth of tacit pedagogic knowledge that teachers simply enact without thinking, and yet this knowledge and these intuitive actions can often constitute successful teaching (see Johansson and Kroksmark, 2004).

Reflection can also enable professionals to go beyond their own individual perspectives to see how their work has an impact on others. It should encourage practitioners to challenge their own assumptions about the client group they work with, and to begin to develop new insights into the purposes of their practice not just for themselves but for their clients (see DeMulder and Rigsby, 2003). It can also encourage a sense of expertise and of valuing our own professional ability in a policy culture that may lead to feelings of demoralization. In other words, it can lead to a stronger sense of our professional self (DeMulder and Rigsby, 2003: 278). This may lead to a stronger sense of self-efficacy and a more robust ability to cope with change and with difficult working situations. In addition, reflection may allow us to examine difficult and challenging situations and discuss these with others to form new understandings of where the challenge lies, and how we could approach similar situations in more effective ways. This is particularly the case where the situation arises from particular moral or ethical considerations.

Giving students, at whatever level, the opportunity to reflect with others on their courses offers them the potential to form supportive relationships, to talk about and to reflect on issues that arise within their practice (see Gould and Masters, 2004). This is where the use of what Gould and Masters (2004) call 'facilitated reflective groups' can be helpful. In advocating these, they recognize that students need support in order to make these groups successful. Gould and Masters (2004: 57) note a tendency in the early stages of their work with mental health nursing students for the group discussions to lose focus, and to fail to make best use of opportunities for reflection. Most notably, in the early discussions deeper levels of reflection were not achieved (Gould and Masters, 2004: 58). It was here that the role of the tutor as facilitator was important in moving students towards more sophisticated reflective practice. Gould and Masters (2004: 59) state that students did become more critically aware during their course, and did try to put elements of their learning into practice. So, in encouraging students to become critically reflective it must be remembered that critical reflection is a skill that needs to be learned, and needs the support of tutors to facilitate reflective opportunities.

There are, then, potential benefits to the use of reflective practice. But in advocating its use we should take care not to adopt a simplistic model of reflection and we should be aware of some of the difficulties associated with its use. In particular we should look at what exactly we are asking practitioners to reflect on and change. In asking them to change their practice we may be asking them to change their understandings of how they practice and of what they regard as their professional role. Ultimately we may be asking individuals to alter their identities and we may be placing too much emphasis on individual change without looking carefully enough at the contexts within which they work. These issues are explored more fully in the following sections.

■ Reflection: changing our practice or changing ourselves?

In debating this issue, it is important not to become polarized (see Heath, 1998). Professional education cannot rest upon one model of practice: it is as unhelpful to claim that reflection should be the overriding basis of professional development as it is to place complete faith in research findings to help us to improve our practice. Professional development needs to be based on a more holistic understanding of what constitutes relevant professional knowledge. Heath (1998: 291) argues that what is required is 'a realistic position and use that will enable successful implementation and the full potential of reflection to be reached in diverse practice settings and contexts'.

Undoubtedly, reflecting on our practice can lead us towards a fuller understanding of our professional role and how we fulfil this. But concerns have been raised, most notably in nursing studies, about whether reflection is being used to change practice or to change our professional identity towards a specific model of the 'good' practitioner (however this is conceived). Reflection is 'extolled as being good for nursing and nurses' (Cotton, 2001: 512), just as it is seen as being empowering for teachers. For many professionals this constitutes an underlying assumption to their initial education and their continuing professional development: you will be a better nurse, teacher, doctor or social worker if you reflect on your practice. But to what extent in current policy is the 'good' practitioner one who follows policy rather than challenges it? Again, there is polarization evident: the 'good' practitioner is a more complex being than either the policy compliant or the 'activist professional' models suggest.

Reflection may well lead to better practice but, as McLaughlin (1999: 11) asks, is a 'reflective teacher *ipso facto* a good teacher? How, for example, is a weak reflective teacher different from a strong unreflective teacher?' He makes two further points that are important. First, it is not straightforward to define 'what counts' as good professional practice (McLaughlin, 1999: 17). Secondly he notes that '[f]lawed reflections, (of whatever kind) can inhibit good practice' (McLaughlin, 1999: 18). Even when carried out diligently and critically, reflection can become an end in itself and so need not affect practice at all. Any claims that reflection leads to improved practice must be examined in terms of whether practitioners can demonstrate lasting positive change for themselves and their clients, and this type of evidence is difficult to find.

Pressure to reflect or willingness to develop?
Reflective practice has now become so much a mainstay of professional education that a culture has been set up where 'not to reflect on ... practice, or to refuse to participate in reflective strategies ... may be seen as unacceptable, unprofessional and unnatural alternatives' (Cotton, 2001: 514). To question reflective practice could lead to being labelled *unprofessional*, or to be seen as not caring about improving professional practice. Newell (1992: 1326) comments that reflective practice is 'regarded by many authors as of particular importance to continuing professional excellence'. Once again, this is an assumption rather than a demonstrable outcome, but it has become an almost unquestioned element in professional education: the root to excellence is through reflection.

Certainly there is evidence that practitioners believe that reflection helps them to improve practice. Burnard's study of nurse educators points to their beliefs about the benefits of reflection (see Burnard, 1995: 1171):

■ improved confidence
■ increased thoughtfulness
■ improved possibility of getting practice 'right'
■ realizing that there is 'no right answer'
■ taking a more systematic approach to practice.

However, since these beliefs are all based upon practitioners' perceptions of improvements, it is difficult to ascertain whether or not objective improvement took place. Moreover, Greenwood (1993: 1183) considers the discrepancies that can arise between what practitioners believe is good practice and what they actually do. Knowledge of 'good' practice may arise through reflection, but within stressful working environments we may not always act in accordance with our beliefs about best professional practice.

This leads into the question of the extent to which we can stand back from our practice and assess it unemotionally, rationally and objectively? In one sense, it is positive that practitioners can form their own meanings of what it is to be a nurse or a teacher. But, in another sense, it can lead to a view of practice which is based on 'common-sense' understandings of professional practice, where theory and research are seen as less valid and less practical than professionals' own view of their work. Of course, reflective exercises should ask professionals to reflect not just on their own experiences, but to underpin those reflections with reading and research. However, in looking at the reflective writing of beginning and experienced professionals, the writing is too often characterized by 'merely thinking about what you're doing' rather than by critique and evaluation that leads to improved practice and service to clients (Burnard, 1995: 1169).

Valid reflection or just another story?
These issues also lead to the question of how meaningful our reflections are especially when they are based on our memory of events, sometimes events that are far removed in time? Newell writes that the

> nature of memory is such that forgetting information takes place all the time ... However, much forgetting is often subject to considerable individual bias. Equally, attention at the time of acquisition is selective ...

> The issues of bias in forgetting and selection at acquisition suggest that accurate reflection may be either impossible or so fundamentally flawed as to be of little value. (Newell, 1992: 1327)

We tend not to remember accurately or fully, nor do we take in the full extent of events at the time, especially where these professional events are stressful (see Newell, 1992: 1327). If we cannot reflect objectively, and we remember events selectively, what value is there to reflection – are we not simply constructing one story of our practice to replace one that already exists? And if we are, does this matter? It may be the case that the difficulties Newell associates with memory are only partially problematic, in that reflection may help us to try to uncover how we remember things and what alternative perspectives we might take when analysing our practice. However, it is also the case that, in advocating the use of story writing and analysis, we guard against what Taylor (2003: 249) calls 'romantic realism' in which practitioners' reflective stories move away from the 'naive realism' that the events they describe have objective truth, but instead 'take on a therapeutic or emancipatory aspect' (Taylor, 2003: 249).

It may be that reflective practice places too much confidence in the 'power of language' (Atkinson, 2004: 379) to effect change. Atkinson (2004: 380) writes that reflective practice assumes that any professional is 'a self-conscious, reflective and hardworking individual whose practice is consciously planned and initiated', which we may well be. But Atkinson questions the role of emotion and subjectivity in how we understand our professional roles, and questions the extent to which reflective practice can give us an adequate platform for exploring our subjective understandings of what we do.

While Atkinson's point is valid, what are the repercussions of asking us to question our emotional and subjective constructs? It may be that in asking us to interrogate our professional values, assumptions and beliefs, reflective practice actually risks undermining our core identity as professionals. At what point can we trust our professional identity and the values and beliefs it rests upon? At what stage in our professional development can we stop interrogating and reinventing our professional selves? We are meant to become empowered, but this implies a shift of power from the institutions and policy towards the individual practitioner (see Gilbert, 1995).

In reality, the strictures placed on professionals by managerialism and by government and institutional policy can make empowerment a tenuous notion. It is also an ambiguous notion: even as authors write of the reflective practitioner or the activist professional, the reality for many is that they develop any autonomy and agency they have within professional cultures that are often based on performance management. The concept of the activist professional takes the notion of the reflective practitioner to new moral heights: not only must the professional reflect, but act to change systems. It is questionable whether this is a helpful premise.

Does reflection empower?

There are, then, issues about whether or not deep reflection on our professional practice and identity constitute a reinventing of the professional self that actually empowers or disempowers. Gilbert (1995) sees empowerment as resting on the question of where power actually lies, and mentions the work of Foucault in looking at disciplinary power (see Gilbert, 1995: 867). For Foucault, power can be both a positive and a negative force: it can be used to dominate and control, or it can act as a potential for agency. Important to this last sense is a critical attitude, or 'the art of not being governed or of not being governed like this and at this price' (Foucault, in Barratt, 2004: 195). Here lies the potential strength of reflection, not as it is often presented in a naive sense of discussing individual practice, but seen as a critical endeavour that takes account of the individual's place in their professional context. For teachers, reflective practice undoubtedly has the potential to enable them to understand the richness and complexity of classroom and school life, and to develop a sense of agency and ownership of their work.

However, it is important to distinguish reflection that is enabling, complex and difficult, from that which has been simplified and used as a tool of managerialism, in particular where it has become a normative expectation of those working towards promotion or undertaking initial education. Reflective practice should not be a further stage in our induction into the normative expectations of what a teacher is or should be. Nor should it be about creating a specific professional type. The danger of this conceptualization of reflective practice is that it can become what Foucault might describe as a technology of the self, where it is used to 'define the individual and control their conduct' (Besley, 2005a: 313). There is a danger within the culture of reflective practice that professional identity becomes something to be continually worked on, 'transformed and improved' as Foucault puts it (1977: 136). Of course, we should not make the mistake of denying the individual agency we have to shape our own professionalism, but it can be difficult to resist and to fully recognize norms of professional practice, especially when building our professional identity and practice at an early stage.

It is also important to recognize forms of reflective practice which become confessional and which focus too much on individual change, rather than on individual development within a professional context. One of the concerns with the dominance of the reflective practice culture is the potential for reflection to be confused with confession (see Gilbert, 2001). As Besley notes (2005b: 369), we live in a 'confessional age' where we should ask, '[w]hat is the effect on us of confessing our selves either publicly or privately?' This last question is relevant to any professional who is expected to engage in reflective practice. We should take care in seeking to understand our professional practice, and as teacher educators in asking others to critically reflect, that we do not become focused on an 'obligation to endlessly reinvent' ourselves as professionals (McNay, 1996: 146).

We have no doubt about the potential of reflective practice, when well used, and when well designed, to allow professionals to renew their ideas about practice and refresh their enthusiasm for their work. Critical reflection can provide us with a powerful learning tool, but it needs to be constructed in a way that recognizes the students' cognitive development, the social dynamics of the workplace, development of professional identity and the multiple factors involved in the specific contexts that professionals find themselves in. The next section looks at an example of the complexities and benefits of reflective practice when used in the professional development of head teachers.

■ The social dynamics of reflective learning

All aspiring head teachers in Scotland now have to undertake the Scottish Qualification for Headship (see Reeves et al., 2005). It is a two-year course of professional development that has at its heart a model of reflective practice that tries to recognize the complexities of meaningful workplace learning and the usefulness of reflection as a focus for learning. It tries to bridge three key theoretical models of CPD:

1 that which focuses on knowledge and skills within the attainment of competences
2 that which sees learning as constructivist with meaning being made by individuals in the context of the institutions they work in (see Reeves et al., 2005: 254)

3 following Lave and Wenger, that which sees professional learning as taking place within the social practices of the workplace (see Reeves et al., 2005: 255).

To this end, participants in the programme undertake taught elements, but there is a strong emphasis on collaborative working and discussion, on reflection, on workplace learning and on understanding that changing individual practice has repercussions beyond the individual practitioner (see Reeves et al., 2001). But the SQH model recognizes that, in and of themselves, each of these three models has its own difficulties. It therefore tries to take elements of each and redevelop them within a new framework for professional development that can take account of situational factors, micro-political issues in the workplace, collegiality and the need for CPD to engage the learner to work towards not just behavioural but conceptual change (see Reeves et al., 2005). Ultimately it aims at 'supported action' within the workplace where professional knowledge is acquired, developed and used (Reeves et al., 2003: 7).

Importantly, Reeves et al. (2005) note the impact of change on professional identity and emotion. They write that

> Changing practice is situated in interaction between the individual and others in the context of the work setting and appears to be characterized by contestation. It is not a purely rational process. The conceptual development of SQH candidates encompassed their professional persona and their relationship to others, it was not simply a matter of developing ideas or acquiring knowledge from self and emotion. The whole person was engaged since at stake was maintaining a respectable professional identity ... (Reeves et al., 2005: 269)

This idea of engaging the whole person is a powerful one, but not without challenge for the individual professional and for the teacher educator, because it uncovers not just the micro-politics of the workplace but the micro-politics and power relations of the learning environment in which the CPD takes place. It also takes on board the recognition that it can be difficult for practitioners to change their practice because institutional practices militate against the transfer of new understandings of practice into reality (see Sparrow et al., 2005).

Leadership

Day's research (2000) with school principals in England, also illustrates the need for effective leadership to be based on reflective practice to some extent. It highlights the fact that these principals engaged in reflection that critiqued their practice and that 'reflection was integral to their success' (Day, 2000: 124). Essential to their efficacy as managers were also a set of core values which promoted not just their own agency but the agency of their staff: fairness, equity and equality of opportunity (Day, 2000: 124). Importantly, in trying to implement these values in the face of the strictures of government policy and the challenges of raising standards, reflection was seen as being crucial to coping with difficulties and complexities of school leadership (Day, 2000: 124).

Power

Reflection can therefore be an important means of identifying core leadership values. Centring CPD for teachers and potential school managers on reflection therefore gives opportunities to think about these issues. But basing CPD on reflective practice also raises questions of power, in particular, concerning the relationship between the professional and the CPD provider/tutor. How do we encourage participants to reflect and engage in change to professional practice within a relationship of equal power (something that can be difficult within the role of CPD provider)? To what extent should the provider be a mentor, a supporter or a 'critical friend' in encouraging critical reflection, particularly when the provider is in the dual role of teacher and assessor? And, when encouraging critical reflection, to what extent does the provider of CPD encourage the student towards professional agency in an ethical manner?

As McNay highlights (1996: 159) issues of power link into moral and ethical concerns: 'To decide whether an individual is being manipulated rather than persuaded involves issues of responsibility and moral considerations about the extent to which it is legitimate to limit or impair the choices of others.' Those who encourage professionals to engage in meaningful reflection have a responsibility to develop an understanding in the practitioner that individual reflection should not lead to change which might limit or impair the choices of others with whom the professional is involved. It is important to recognize the perspectives of those we work with when we reflect, and to try to listen to what they say and what they want as we strive to become better practitioners. It is important to ask ourselves as we reflect or as we encourage reflection in others, do we listen, or do we overpower the perspectives of those we work with and work for? (See Miehls and Moffat, 2000.)

The development of the Scottish Qualification for Headship, and the work of Day with school leaders, serve as a reminder that reflective practice can enable participants to renew their conceptual understanding of their professional roles at what can be a challenging time: the move into, or the further development of, a leadership role. It also serves to show the multiple levels involved in changing practice. The work of Reeves et al. (2005: 270)

> raises doubts about the whole idea that 'changing' individuals is an adequate basis for seeking to change practice. It shows that there is a complex dynamic involved where one individual cannot change what she does without the acquiescence, compliance and participation of others … Concentrating on developing practitioner competence as solely an individual characteristic needs to be challenged …

Changing the individual is not enough: if we are to improve learning for pupils in our schools then we must focus on change at school level, and this is a complex process. Any process of individual reflection, change and development needs to take account of the cultural factors at work in institutions such as schools and hospitals, and to take account of how the individual's professional identity meshes with that culture or otherwise (see Reeves et al., 2003: 20).

■ Conclusion

It is important, then, to look at wider contexts for professional development: how to implement policy but retain ownership of teaching work; how to improve individual practice within the school as an organization; how to ensure that reflection leads to sustained efforts to improve learning for all pupils. It may be that to focus on individual teacher development is to miss the opportunity to think about what the school can do to further pupil learning and to encourage the professional development of its teachers.

In the next chapter we focus on this issue: teachers do not work in isolation, and if they are to develop professionally they need to have support within their schools to do so. And in looking at how children's learning experiences can be improved, the school policy and forms of management need to be the focus as much as what teachers do in their classrooms. It may be that current policy initiatives that stress instrumental approaches to learning as a means to raise standards miss the point of the school as a learning organization and so place too much emphasis on individual teacher change rather than on how teaching takes place within the social dynamics of schools.

6 Teacher professional identity: the organizational context

Chapter outline

The focus of this chapter is on professionalism and identity within an organizational context. Here we examine the role and responsibilities of the teacher within the whole school: what is expected of teachers and where tensions might lie between teachers exercising their professional judgement and the demands of organizational policies and procedures. We begin by looking at the issue of professionalism and the organization, and then consider the implications of this discussion for the position of teachers. Of critical importance here is the changing context of the school and evolving ideas of 'distributed leadership' and 'professional learning communities' in which teachers work alongside other professionals and para-professionals to support the learning of pupils. We consider the impact of these trends for the identity and development of teachers.

Keywords

■ The school as an organization

■ Organizational values

■ Professional learning communities

■ Distributed leadership

■ Para-professionalism and inter-professionalism

■ Professionalism and the organization

In the previous chapter we considered some of the tensions between government policy and classroom realities. This points to the need to understand teacher professionalism and identity as something that is shaped by, and operates within, different pressures and contexts. In this chapter, the organizational context is defined as the specific institution in which a teacher is employed. However, the school does not stand in isolation. We also need to be aware of the influences exerted by the wider local and national systems on the school's policies and programmes and, so, on the practice of teachers.

Ideas about professionalism have very much rested on the construct of the individual basing her/his professional judgement and behaviour on certain ethical considerations. The individual professional here is accountable to the client for the actions which are taken and will be guided by the code of conduct of their appropriate professional regulatory body. From the previous discussion it is clear that this focus on the practice and accountability of the individual is an important dynamic. However, we must acknowledge that most professionals today practise within an organizational context; whether this be a business or commercial institution or a public sector service such as health or education. Thus, we need to consider the impact of this organizational context on the exercise of professionalism. On the one hand, there is a view that the organizational context reduces individual professional agency with regard to the ability to make decisions. This is particularly the case in an era where institutional policies are based on ideas of performance. On the other hand, there are substantial benefits from conceiving of the teacher as someone who works collectively with other professionals to achieve the task of educating children and young people.

Much of what has been written about teachers' professionalism has been within a construction of the school characterized by its roles and structures. However, organizations are not simply about roles, systems and structures, accountability and policy implementation. More recent discussions about schools have emphasized the social dimensions of organizations – what Sergiovanni (1999: 17), borrowing from Habermas (1987), calls the 'lifeworlds' in contrast to the 'systemsworlds' or organizational structures.

Increasingly when we consider the issues of professional identity and development we are having to consider the importance of community, social processes of change, the development of professional discourses and the production of professional knowledge; and the organization provides a very powerful site of learning for professionals. Organizations are about interaction and relationships through which the purpose of the organization must be achieved. This social dimension of organizational life is critical in the exercise of professionalism and the definition of what it means to be a teacher. In this chapter we will explore how evolving organizational context of the school is impacting on teacher identity and development.

■ The organizational context

If we are to pose the question of whether teachers can forge new professional identities that can help them to capture or recapture ownership of their profession, we need to consider this against the organizational context. First, though, we need to explore further what is meant by 'organizational contexts' (Figure 6.1). In education, the organizational context for teachers is dynamic, complex and multilayered. When we talk of the organizational context we might mean the immediate department or unit of the school in which an individual teacher works because there is no doubt that this is an important context. For teachers, whether it is a stage in the primary school such as upper or early stages, or the department or faculty in a secondary school, this is an important context in the professional life of an individual teacher for a number of reasons. First, it is here on a day-to-day basis that the regular contacts are made with those staff who undertake similar roles or areas of expertise; where the people with whom the teacher will share the social times of the school day such as break times; where the teacher will work on collaborative teaching activities. Secondly, for many individual teachers this location is also part of their identity: 'I am a early years teacher' or 'I am a

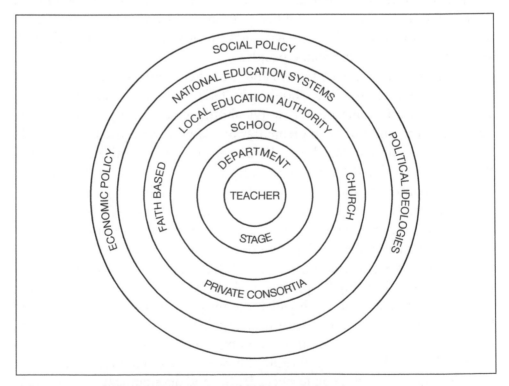

Figure 6.1 ■ The organizational context of the teacher

geography teacher'. However, the workings of these sub-units are shaped by the wider organizational context of the school. We need, then, to consider the position of the teacher within the wider school setting. To examine this we have to conceive of the school as an organization within wider educational systems.

Schools in the UK exist within wider contexts, whether as part of a local education authority, private consortium, church or faith provision, and within one of the national educational systems. These wider contexts make demands on individual teachers as well as staff collectively in schools. In this wider educational system there exist policy frameworks within which schools must operate and which, in turn, teachers are expected to work towards.

It is often within these relationships between policy decisions and initiatives at governmental level – whether local or national – and the practice and location of individual teachers working within a specific school, that tensions can arise. The policy frameworks and priorities of the national governments within the UK should not be seen as distant from the work of the individual practitioner in their classroom, but they have a significant influence on the curriculum and its delivery. These policies have included areas such as curriculum, assessment, pedagogy and behaviour management, and very much seek to impact on the day-to-day work of the teacher. Attention in recent policy initiatives has also moved into issues relating to the role and position of the teacher, both individually and as a profession. In both Scotland and England there have been significant changes instigated nationally to the career structure for teachers: in England the introduction of threshold payments (DfES, 2005b) and in Scotland the post-McCrone Agreement (SEED, 2001), both of which we will consider later.

■ The teacher in the school

Across the UK there are descriptions of what it means to be a teacher enshrined in competence or benchmark frameworks designed to assess performance particularly of those entering the profession. By implication the areas of competence mapped in these various frameworks are also expected of experienced teachers. An important aspect emphasized in these frameworks is the collegiate role of the teacher working with other teachers and with other professionals. In the *Statement of Professional Values* from the General Teaching Council for England (GTCE) (2004b: 2) the role of the teacher working with other teachers and with other professionals is underlined:

Colleagues

Teachers support, and cooperate with, their colleagues to maintain effective and professional working relationships. They share their views, experience and expertise with colleagues, seeking and valuing the ideas and insights of others, for the benefit of pupils. They are sensitive to the need, where appropriate, for confidentiality.

Other professionals

Teachers recognise the contribution provided by, and needed from other professionals in the learning process. They collaborate with others, as appropriate, in the best interests of the pupil and the school.

Similar statements are to be found in *The Professional Code for Teachers* from the General Teaching Council for Wales (GTCW) (2002) and in the Scottish framework, *The Standard for Full Registration* (General Teaching Council for Scotland, 2002). These ideas inform the activities expected of teachers across the UK. If we take these three documents we can see some common themes that are shaping the position and expectations made of teachers (Table 6.1).

Table 6.1 ■ The teacher in the school context

Teachers work collegially with other teachers
Teachers contribute to the corporate life of the school
Teachers work with other professionals and support staff in the classroom
Teaches work with other professionals in the wider school context
Teachers are also part of the school and its partnership with the wider community

Each of the areas is concerned with the teacher's wider role within the school organization. We need, therefore, to consider what we mean by the school as an 'organization'.

■ The school as an organization

The term 'organization' can be defined in various ways. Schein (1980: 15), who is interested in the psychology of organizations, provides a broad definition of an organization: '[a]n organization is the planned co-ordination of the activities of a number of people for the achievement of some common, explicit purpose or goal, through division of labour and function and through a hierarchy of authority and responsibility'.

We can see how this fits with the concept of a school: there is the co-ordination of the activities of teachers and pupils alike to achieve the common goal of pupil learning, and these activities are managed through a clear school management structure. Schein's definition provides an outline of the basic structure or system of an organization. However, we know from our everyday experiences in any educational establishment that organizations are more complex because they are made up of people who come with a range of attitudes, motivations, personal goals and ways of interacting with each other. Handy (1981: 18) highlights the importance of the interaction between the people within an organization. Thus we can see two significant aspects of an organization: first, the collection of individuals – the people dimension – and, secondly, the political systems through which the collection of individuals come together. The political systems of an organization will have defined boundaries, goals and values, administrative mechanisms and hierarchies of power. The people dimension and the political dimension are held together by a third idea, that of power and influence. It is through the exercise of power and influence that a 'psychological contract' is established. This can be defined as the set of ways of working that individuals implicitly or explicitly agree to follow in order that through individual and collective action the goals are achieved within the terms of the organization.

In these ideas put forward by Schein and Handy, we can see how individual teachers are influenced by and potentially able to influence others within the school as an organization. The 'psychological contract' that Handy talks about is much more than simply the contract a teacher has in terms of employment, because it is also about a teacher's motivation: her/his attitudes, willingness and commitment to this particular setting. Thus when we consider a school's culture we are looking at far more than the systems and structures that exist. A school's culture is about the quality of the interactions, the attitudes and emotions that are expressed by members of the organization that shape the day-to-day experience of life in that particular school.

We might see the organizational context as something that has a limiting effect on an individual teacher and the exercising of their professionalism: both in terms of the employment contract and now this psychological contract. There are certain behaviours and functions that teachers are expected to not just 'do' but to 'buy into'. In other words, teachers are expected to make a personal commitment particularly to the expressed goals and purposes of the institution. Inevitably, working in an organizational context can pose specific dilemmas for individual professionals.

■ The individual and the organization

Current expectations on teachers place them firmly within the school as an organization and we have to consider what tensions and potentials emerge when we view the exercise of professionalism within the context of a school. The idea of 'accountability' is, in the first instance, within the demands of the school and we have to consider whether an organization reduces individual professional agency by limiting the ability to make decisions, particularly in an environment where increasingly policy is based on ideas of performance. In some of the most challenging dilemmas for teachers, particularly those dealing with vulnerable young people, there are significant limitations imposed by the policies and procedures of the organization. This is partly for the protection of the pupil and partly for the professionals who have to work with them. However, policies cover all areas of professional practice. A school will have policies on a range of areas that very much determine the daily life of the classroom and the work of the teacher (Table 6.2).

Table 6.2 ■ Policy and practice

Area	Example of prescribed practice
Planning learning	A monthly plan using a specific format must be completed
The curricular programme	Specific units and materials to be completed in a set period
The assessment process	Use of check-up tests weekly
Teaching strategies	Whole-class interactive teaching for numeracy
Grouping of pupils	Use of setting in science
Classroom management	Guidelines on layout and display
Behaviour management	Use of points scheme as a reward

Policies frequently provide useful guidelines to support the complex activities of teaching and learning in the classroom. However, what should a teacher do when she/he is fundamentally at odds with a particular policy? This disagreement is often characterized as a teacher being 'awkward' or 'old-fashioned' but we have to recognize that, in some instances at least, the disagreement may have a profound basis. Let us consider some scenarios:

Scenario 1 A teacher does not agree with the policy on behaviour management in which there are a limited range of reprimands that can be used. This she feels does children a true disservice. To her mind (and honest belief) it does not allow the children to develop an understanding of the consequences of their own actions and decisions, and so she has introduced a number of punishments in her classroom.

Scenario 2 The school has a policy for setting in mathematics with pupils in the upper stages but the teacher feels that this is fundamentally flawed, seeing it as 'streaming by the back door'. He, therefore, has indicated that his class will not be part of the setting programme.

Scenario 3 A teacher has begun to change the reading programme for a group of pupils because she feels that the materials deal with relationships in a way that is inappropriate for pupils of that age. The new material covers many areas in the set programme but there are some significant gaps.

Scenario 4 The school working group has developed a programme which includes using single-gender classes with pupils in the middle years of the secondary school. However, one teacher disagrees with this practice as he believes boys and girls need to learn to be able to work productively together. He has read up on the issue and feels there is no evidence to support this practice.

In each situation, from their standpoint, the teacher is genuinely trying to act in the learning interests of a specific group of pupils whether it is by using a particular approach to behaviour management, pupil grouping or selecting curricular material (see also, Table 6.3). On the other hand, when we are considering the whole school and the needs of all pupils, we do need some overall structure to ensure that there is a sense of progression, equity and success for all pupils, and fairness in the treatment of all staff. These scenarios raise questions about:

■ the right of pupils to expect that teachers' behaviour and decisions will confirm to a prescribed standard
■ teachers' ability to make decisions based on their own beliefs, values and expectations
■ expectations of teachers in relation to mutual support and co-operation
■ expectations of the management of the school that school policy and guidelines will be followed to ensure consistency
■ the expectations of parents that the published school policies will be followed.

Table 6.3 ■ Scenarios

Scenario	Questions
1	Is a teacher able to act on his/her own beliefs that might be counter to the professional values or practices?
2	Can an individual teacher, who has a different ideological stance, make this decision?
3	Can a teacher move beyond the set curricular programme and draw on material that, in her evaluation, is 'more suitable'?
4	Where does one teacher's considered professional judgement sit in relation to the school's policy?

In each scenario there has been sets of competing sets of values seeking 'the best interests of the pupil' (Shapiro and Stefkovich, 2001: 24). Bruner (1990: 29) points to the importance of values within a social setting:

> [Values] are communal and consequential in terms of our relations to a cultural community. They fulfil functions for us in that community. The values underlying a way of life ... Are only lightly open to 'radical reflection.' They become incorporated into one's self identity and at the same time, they locate one in a culture.

Nevertheless values and beliefs are contested at a societal level, within the profession and within specific institutions. For teachers making choices and decisions about their professional practice there are competing sets of values (Table 6.4).

Each of the scenarios raises the question of whether an individual teacher can ignore a policy decision or accepted school practice because it does not match what they see as important. There is no easy answer to this. As society has become more diverse, schools have become more explicit in what they stand for and what they seek to achieve. Schools now have mission statements and sets of aims that will be informed by different viewpoints – for example, the immediate community the school serves, whether the school has areas of curriculum specialism or provides faith-based education. Such statements are intended to make explicit the position of the school and the values it operates on. There is no doubt that these statements are potentially very powerful. Each of us will have our own values system that will be a mixture of personal belief, professional ideas and unquestioned assumptions. However, now, to be part of a school community, teachers are asked to make explicit and to be part of an organization based on a particular set of values.

Table 6.4 ■ Competing values

The code of the profession	The statements from the General Teaching Council
The individual teacher's personal values	Values derived from the teacher's own religious or political or social beliefs
The individual teacher's professional code	How the teacher constructs her/his professional responsibilities
The values of the school	The statement of values in the school's mission and aims
The values of the wider community	The personal, political, religious or social beliefs of members of the local community – though these may very well differ significantly within the community

The scenarios depict the individual standing out against the policies of the school. However, we should be wary of constructing a model of the professional teacher as always being at odds with the institution and instead consider more closely the place of teachers within the school and their contribution to and ownership of the aims, policies, practices and development of the school.

■ The teacher and the school

In previous chapters we have mapped out the waves of changes in education in the late 1980s and 1990s across the UK. Thus in England and Wales there was the introduction of the National Curriculum, testing and the publication of results on a school-by-school basis – the league tables. In Scotland, though the political context was very different, there were similar developments with the introduction of the 5–14 Curriculum, national testing and the publication of school examination results. Centralized policy-making continues today. In England schools are expected to take forward a range of national policy initiatives which very much deal with the day-to-day work in classrooms from central government – such as the literacy strategy – while in Scotland there is the range of published national priorities arising from the Standards in Scotland's Schools Act 2000, which schools must address.

The late 1980s and early 1990s saw also the establishment of management structures such as school development planning, devolved resource management and teacher appraisal and development. These systems were intended to enable schools to become more 'self-managing' (Caldwell and Spinks,

1988). However, this does not mean that schools were to become completely independent. There has been a paradoxical move: while work was going on setting up systems for self-management there was an increasing array of policies and frameworks that school managers had to ensure were implemented. The line management systems in schools designed to ensure the implementation of national policy have had a cost. The divide between management and teaching creates a separation of managers from the core business of any school, the teaching and learning processes, and teachers from the processes of decision-making about teaching and learning in the school.

The questions then are: what has been the impact of these developments on the individual teacher and the exercise of her/his professionalism within an organizational context? Do the layers of management structures detract from the individual teacher's ability to exercise her/his professional practice? Do these systems place the individual teacher as an employee within an organization whose sole function – for which she/he is accountable – is to implement the range of policies and guidelines?

Job satisfaction and motivation

To see an organization simply as limiting an individual teacher's autonomy to act in relation to her/his own beliefs and values overlooks some of the considerable benefits and opportunities that the organizational context of the school can provide for an individual teacher. Part of the psychological contract we looked at earlier is about commitment and support to the individual as well as the individual making a commitment to the organization. We can see this particularly in aspects such as job satisfaction and morale and in opportunities to develop and to progress in their career as a teacher.

There is no doubt that the demands of running a classroom or a school are heavy, often both physically and psychologically; but teachers are motivated to take on these tasks and they obviously derive a sense of achievement and satisfaction from them. As we have seen from our discussions in Section A, there have been debates and campaigns by the teaching unions to ensure a professional level of pay. Pay, however, is only part of *any* discussion about job satisfaction and motivation. Issues like pay and working conditions are not the simple keys to enhancing job satisfaction. Evans (1999) drawing from Herzberg's motivation-hygiene theory (1968) argues that when teachers are dissatisfied with pay and working conditions this has a negative effect; but when conditions are improved there is not a commensurate rise in job satis-faction. Other factors are far more significant, and that is why the organizational context becomes so important. To explain this we need to go to ideas about human motivation, particularly Maslow's (1954) hierarchy of needs in which the following are placed as the two uppermost needs. First, there are esteem needs: we need to know we are valued and we value our-selves. Secondly, there are self-actualization needs: we need opportunities to realize our potential, to be stimulated, and to seek and achieve challenges.

If we look at an organization such as a school, it has a fundamental role to play in enabling individuals – both teachers and pupils – to meet their needs in terms of esteem and self-actualization. A successful organization will be one where an individual feels valued and believes that she/he is given opportunities for growth and development. The range of initiatives and poli-cies from central and local government are often pointed to as the cause of 'low teacher morale'. However, the climate of the school, Evans (1999: 16) argues, has a much more powerful influence:

> The reason why it is school-specific issues, situations and circumstances that evidently take precedence as morale- motivation- and job satisfaction-influ-encing factors is that they constitute teachers' working lives. It is the context-specific level that teachers carry out their work. Centrally-initiated conditions, or indeed any conditions that emanate from outside the contexts in which teachers work, only become real for, and meaningful and relevant to, teachers when they become contextualised. Until they are effected within the contexts in which teachers work, such conditions are non-operational: they exist only in abstract forms as ideas, principles or rhetoric. They do not constitute reality.

We need to re-conceive what we mean by a school by highlighting the social aspects of school life. Here we have to get a balance between the area an individual teacher is responsible for and in which she/he has the right/responsibility to make decisions, and the overall processes of learn-ing and the impact of a pupil's cumulative experiences across the school. It is important that individual teachers have a real focus on the area they are working in every day, whether this is with a particular age group or a particular subject. However teachers also need to be aware of, and increasingly actively involved in, the development of the whole school in shaping provision for learners. If we compartmentalize pupils' learning, whether by age, stage or subject, and there is little attention paid to the holistic nature of pupils' development, their experience will be fragmented and progress will be slower.

School community and culture

How, then, do we enable teachers to develop this more holistic approach to the development of pupils throughout their career in the school? We need to foreground another view that the organization is not simply about accountability and policy implementation, particularly in a top-down model of accountability. Fullan (1992: 39) writes of 'interactive professionalism' with teachers not working as isolated individuals but working collegially and contributing to the whole school. Increasingly we are having to consider the importance of community, social processes of change, the development of professional discourses and the production of professional knowledge: and the organization provides a very powerful site of learning for professionals. There are other aspects that are important in terms of teacher professionalism, identity and development, including the ethos of the school and the relationships with pupils and other teachers, the standing of the school in its local community and wider perceptions of the role of the teacher.

School culture has a profound effect on the learners' view of themselves and their learning. School culture will also have a profound effect on teachers and their perception of their role particularly in taking forward change that will enhance the learning experiences of the pupils. Stoll and Fink (1996) cite among the ten cultural norms of an improving school the following, which focus on the relationships between members of the school, especially between the professionals working within that context: collegiality, support, mutual respect, openness, celebration and humour.

Viewing a school as a community is not just about people 'being nice to one another' and generally 'getting along'. This is a form of 'cosy consensus' which actually detracts from the task of the school to provide effective learning experiences to the young people. Instead, there has to be a clear sense of the shared values of all who are members of the school community. Sergiovanni (2003: 16) argues that:

Schools that resemble institutions have central zones of values and beliefs that take on sacred characteristics. As repositories of values, these central zones are the sources of identity for parents, teachers and students from which their school lives become meaningful. Meaningfulness leads to elevated levels of commitment to the school, greater effort, tighter connections for everyone, and more intensive academic engagement for students – all of which are virtues in themselves but have added value of resulting in heightened levels of student performance and increased academic performance.

Rather than have the situation of a teacher being at odds with a particular policy or practice which has come from 'government policy', the teacher should have an active role in the school, debating and defining policies, practices and their underpinning values.

■ Professional learning communities

More recently there have been moves towards flatter organizational structures in schools and to the development of ideas about 'distributing leadership practice' (Spillane et al., 2005). Here we need to rethink what we mean by leadership not as line management or administration but, instead, as the collective task of supporting, developing and enhancing the learning experiences of pupils. There needs to be a relationship between an individual teacher's accountability to undertake the task of teaching along specific lines and the opportunities they have to develop and contribute to the school's policy-making and development processes. There are substantial benefits from conceiving teachers not just as individual professionals left to make decisions or take action but, instead, as working collegially with other staff to contribute to the framework of expressed organizational values, policies and procedures.

Barth (2001) makes a distinction between 'learning-impoverished' and 'learning-rich schools'. In this learning environment the key is not just about teachers learning but teachers learning *together*. This is a process centred on professional practice. As Cordingley et al. (2005: 89) suggest, collaboration between teachers is about trying out ideas and practice – the 'active experimentation' helps to change practice and secure teachers' commitment to the projects within the school's development agenda. The idea that schools should be focusing on the learning of all its members has increasing currency and is characterized as 'professional learning communities': '[i]t is thought that in professional learning communities, teachers and school leaders, collaborating with and supported by support staff, exercise professional judgements, for example about the best use of evidence and research for improving learning and teaching, within an agreed accountability framework' (Stoll and Bolam, 2005: 54).

The idea of building a learning community to enhance the learning experiences of pupils is becoming a pivotal idea in the national education systems in the UK. Thus the Teachers' Agreement Communications Team (TACT, 2004: 18) in Scotland argue that a need to focus 'on leadership capacity within the whole organization, and not just on the traditional figure of the headteachers, improves the school's capacity to deliver better performance, higher levels of motivation and sustainable development'.

The changing role of the teacher

What is emerging here is the changing position role of the teacher in leading the development agenda of the school. Teachers have always been expected to play some sort of collective role but now there is a fundamental change in the way schools are to be managed to enable teachers to play this role productively. This change evident in schools across the UK is aptly illustrated by the McCrone Agreement (SEED, 2001a: annex D) in Scotland in which there is a clear statement about the responsibility and right of teachers to participate in whole school development processes:

> Teachers have a right and an obligation to contribute to the process by which national and local priorities are determined. Programmes of change will require the full participation of staff at establishment level in decisions about the pace of change.

> … All teachers will have the right to be fully involved in the development of the plan and to be consulted on their contribution to the plan, and the responsibility for realising the school's development priorities. If a plan requires to be reviewed to take account of individual or collective circumstances, staff will be involved in any review as appropriate.

Leadership and management can be constructed in broad terms as 'the way things are organized and the relationship between the different levels of management/activity in the school'. Within this a critical distinction could be made between strategic, personnel and resource management at senior and middle management level, and the leadership of learning which is to be a more distributed function across all staff in the school. To facilitate and exploit – in the best sense – teachers' contribution to the whole school, we need to consider the transformation of leadership processes across the school. This, however, is not an easy task.

In the policy document *Time for Standards* (DfES, 2002: 27) in England on remodelling the workforce in schools, the head teacher is being characterized as 'a leader of leaders':

> To achieve their full potential, teachers need to work in a school that is creative, enabling and flexible. And the biggest influence is the Head. Every teacher is a leader in the classroom. Every Head must be the leader of these leaders. And the Head's greatest task is the motivation and deployment of their key resource: staff.

However, Rayner and Gunter (2005: 152) argue that this policy 'retains and strengthens hierarchical leadership principally located in the headteacher'. We can see a tension between the traditional type of hierarchical leadership and ideas about teachers being leaders: distributed leadership. There are various ways of interpreting what we mean by distributed leadership but perhaps the most useful for our purposes here is the description put forward by Spillane et al. (2005: 37) in which 'leadership [is] distributed in the interactive web of leaders, followers and situation'. There are different ways in which leadership practice is 'stretched over leaders, followers and situations'.

Despite their reservations Rayner and Gunter (2005: 160), reporting on the Transforming the School Workforce (TSW) project, give illustrations of the types of practices that enable the leadership to be distributed through the involvement of teachers within change management groups in the school:

> Our work in the case study schools would suggest that new attitudes to professionality and working practices for development resulted in many of the achievements. This, to such an extent, that there is evidence of a set of professional practices, attitudes and structures emerging that will demand new forms of educational leadership. Complexity, change and curriculum as process form an interesting mix of structural forces combining to challenge traditional power structures inside and outside of the school setting.

As they suggest, these processes are having a significant impact on the role and position of the teacher and this process of transformation is not without tensions. There are questions about the legitimacy of collegiate approaches, particularly the role of non-promoted staff and those in management posts. Though the involvement of teachers in the decision-making processes is valuable there has to be a note of caution because this is not teachers taking over 'management functions' but, instead, must be clearly focused on leading learning. As Timperley (2005: 417) argues:

> [d]istributing leadership over more people is a risky business and may result in the greater distribution of incompetence. *I suggest that increasing the distribution of leadership is only desirable if the quality of the leadership activities contributes to assisting teachers to provide more effective instruction to their students, and it is on these qualities that we should focus.*
> (Original emphasis)

■ Connected practice

We have looked at the changing position of teachers in relation to their contribution to the whole school. However, this is only one aspect of the development of professional learning communities. Professional learning communities will involve a range of other professionals who are contributing to the support of pupils. Teachers are now working collegially with other professionals. This development places not only new demands on the teacher, but also positions the teacher differently. Further, this development raises questions about what new skills, attributes and practices are demanded of the teacher.

The move towards 'connected practice' between different educational, health and welfare agencies challenges the position of the teacher in potentially quite radical ways. The publication of *Every Child Matters* (HMG, 2004: 13) in England is having a major impact on the role and position of the teacher, laying the foundations for far greater collaborative practice across different services:

Children's trust arrangements will have four essential components:

■ professionals enabled and encouraged to work together in more integrated front-line services, built around the needs of children and young people;

- common processes which are designed to create and underpin joint working;
- a planning and commissioning framework which brings together agencies' planning, supported as appropriate by the pooling of resources, and ensures key priorities are identified and addressed, and
- strong inter-agency governance arrangements, in which shared ownership is coupled with clear accountability.

Increasingly this has meant that decisions not just about a child's care but also her/his education are taken by educational professionals working alongside social workers, health-care workers and legal professionals. A similar programme has been set up in Scotland to bring together a range of areas under the idea of 'Children's Services' (SEED, 2001a: 53) both at local authority level and at school level, particularly with the establishment of new community schools which 'are fundamental to the Executive's aims to raise educational attainment and promote social justice. Central to the approach is the integrated provision of school education, family support and health services'.

Where multi-agencies are involved with pupils who, for a variety of social, psychological and physical reasons, may have additional support needs, learning plans are drawn collaboratively with teachers working with other professionals, with the child or young person and their family or carer. This policy of integration and connected practice has reshaped the role of the teacher from someone who is concerned solely with the learning processes within the classroom to one who collaborates with other professionals to make decisions that will shape the learning experiences of the child

In the Scottish report, *For Scotland's Children* (SEED, 2004b: 81) which surveyed different groups – both from professions and from communities – one of the suggestions put forward by some to replace existing professions with 'a new profession was that covered by social workers/guidance teachers/health visitors' whose primary role would be to work with the young person and their family to ensure their educational progress through their ongoing care and welfare. Though this view has not been acted upon, it does pose an interesting possibility and illustrates how in this new policy environment the role and practice of the teacher are in a state of flux.

Inter-agency working is a major challenge to teachers and the teaching profession as a whole. McCulloch et al. (2004), in reviewing the new community schools, found that these were largely perceived as educational initiatives in which any other services were seen as 'add-ons' and that other professions often regarded as 'support' staff rather than professionals with equal standing. As Glaister and Glaister (2005) suggest, new ways of working are now being demanded of teachers to be able to communicate and practise in a trustful and productive way with other professionals concerned with the holistic development of the child or young person.

■ Conclusion

In this chapter we have considered the issue of teacher development and identity within the organizational context of the school. In considering the development of the teacher as an autonomous professional we have argued for this being about teacher agency to undertake their professional responsibilities rather than practise as an isolated individual. We need to reject the idea that it is the autonomous professional against the organization but, instead, look to the organizational context as one in which the teacher, alongside other professionals, works towards achieving what is in the best interests of the child or young person. However, this is making new demands on teachers who will have to develop new skills, new understandings and new ways of working in the wider school context. There are also significant changes within the setting of the classroom which raise questions about the position and development of the teacher, which are considered in the next chapter.

7 Towards leadership for learning

Chapter outline

In this chapter the changing role of the teacher in the context of the classroom is examined. A range of policy initiatives from the various educational systems in the UK is explored in order to identify specific trends that are reshaping and repositioning the teacher. Among those explored are the impact of inclusive education and diversity, the development of citizens of the future, the impact of our growing understanding of the potential of e-learning and of the nature of the learning process. We also consider the impact of para-professionalism and the evolving concept of 'teacher leadership'.

Keywords

- The inclusive classroom
- The democratic classroom
- Learner agency
- The e-classroom
- Para-professionalism
- Teacher leadership

■ Introduction

In the previous chapter, we considered the position of the teacher within the school context, noting both the tensions and opportunities for development provided by this wider organizational setting. In this chapter we turn our attention to the context of the classroom. The wider school context and that of the classroom are interlinked in terms of teacher identity, development and practice, but we have to acknowledge the centrality of classroom experiences in teachers' identity and development. In some respects the classroom of today bears a resemblance to the classroom of the nineteenth century: a number of children or young people broadly segregated by age are taught by the single adult present – the teacher. However, these are superficial similarities and there are some qualitative differences between the setting of the traditional classroom and the contemporary one, and very different demands are made on the teachers of today from those made on previous generations of teachers. While ideas such as 'distributed leadership' (Spillane et al., 2005) or 'teacher leadership' (Harris and Muijs, 2005) signal a role for the teacher beyond the classroom, these ideas also mark the evolution of the role and position of the teacher within the classroom where the teacher can be seen as 'leading learning'.

There are several ways in which the classroom is changing significantly and the range of pressures and influences include:

- wider social changes
- greater understanding of the nature of learning in the classroom
- technological developments
- changing profile of staff in the school.

There is also the direct influence of educational policy by central government. In each of the national educational systems in the UK, there are overarching policy documents such as *Higher Standards: Better Schools for All* (HMG, 2005) and *Ambitious, Excellent Schools* (SEED, 2004a) in Scotland. In Wales a vision and a strategic plan for the development of education is laid out in *The Learning Country* (National Assembly of Wales, 2001). However, these proposals are not distant from the everyday practices of a teacher because the classroom is as much subject to political policy as the school. The school might act as a buffer, providing the setting in which specific initiatives can be tailored to match local circumstances, but the ambitions of policy directives can only be realized through change in the day-to-day processes of the classroom. It is in this location that differences are made to the learning of our children.

Political scrutiny and debate about the pedagogic practice of teachers is, however, not a new phenomenon. Recent strategies such as the literacy hour and numeracy hour in English and Welsh schools are located in a long line of policy directives that specify pedagogic practices to be adopted by teachers in their classrooms. Indeed, there is still a generation of teachers in schools today who recall the charged debates about progressive teaching methods in the 1960s and 1970s. The differences now are, first, the range of detailed material readily available to all teachers and, second, the closer monitoring of practice in classrooms through the use of information on pupil attainment and through the development of policy and management systems within schools. Schools now have a range of detailed policies on different aspects of classroom practice and these will have be developed drawing upon the substantial range of national and local advice and guidelines that are available. Further, a teacher's practice is scrutinized through management systems such as professional review and monitoring of classroom processes, and pupil attainment and the evaluation of curricular programmes.

Given the level of detail found in policy and guidelines, it would be easy to conceive the teacher as passive and her only role largely that of policy implementation. If this is the case, then the only alternative for teachers is to resist these policies. However, as we have argued previously, that would be a very limited response. It is one of retreat that only serves to isolate the teacher, especially from colleagues within the professional community of the school and from the support and development networks they provide. We should be looking for opportunities for teachers to become more engaged in the decision-making and development processes in relation to learning in the school and in the classroom.

We have noted that there have been significant changes in education: governance, management systems and prescriptive curricular programmes have reshaped schools in order to make education more efficient as a public service. In this chapter we consider how the role and position of the teacher is the classroom is evolving. To do so we draw largely on policies and guidelines and evaluations from the various educational systems in the UK. This is by no means a comprehensive survey but is intended to identify the trends in policy and in the political imagination that are having a significant bearing on the role and practice of teachers in classroom. There are a number of different trends that are impacting on the role of the teacher:

- the inclusive classroom
- the classroom in a democratic society
- the changing position of the learner

- learning about learning
- the e-classroom
- para-professionals in the classroom
- teacher leadership.

■ The inclusive classroom

Educational policy is forged against a backdrop of wider social and economic development. As we move towards a knowledge economy in the UK, economic strategy and social policy have become deeply meshed and the political vision is very much one of having to utilize the abilities and potential of all – a matter of both social justice and economic prosperity.

> For just as it will be the nations that fail to open up opportunity, get the best out of their people, fail to tap the potential of all its citizens that will rapidly fall behind, so it is also true that the countries that will succeed best in the global economy will be those that bring out the best talents of all no matter their birth, race, sex or background. (Brown, 2005: n.p.)

If this ambition of tapping the potential of all is to be achieved, the central task of the teacher in the classroom is to remove any barriers to learning being experienced by either individual pupils or groups of pupils from a particular background, and to create genuine inclusive education.

We need to look closely at the term 'inclusive education'. This term is often used to refer to the inclusion of pupils with specific learning or support needs within mainstream education. This is an extremely important aspect and has had a significant impact on life in the classroom, with teachers now working with a wide range of children or young people some of whom will have identifiable additional support needs, whether these be physical, social and emotional or intellectual. However, inclusive education is far wider than this and relates to the role of public education in bringing about social justice and equity. Classrooms are becoming more diverse in terms of pupils' cultural and ethnic background, religious belief, family background, and learning and support needs. Inclusive education is making significant demands on teachers in terms of their own understandings and practice. The role of the teacher has become more complex and teachers need to develop:

- cultural literacy – being aware of, valuing different religious and cultural practices
- social awareness of the greater diversity in lifestyle and family patterns
- greater knowledge about the range of learning and support needs individual pupils or groups of pupils may have
- competence in diagnosing and addressing very varied learning and support needs.

We first look at the issues of diversity in relation to cultural practices, religious belief and lifestyle, and then move on to consider issues related to the inclusion of pupils with different learning and support needs, in line with a 'presumption of mainstream' for all pupils (Scottish Executive, 2000).

Diversity of culture, religions and lifestyles

Being genuinely inclusive means teachers developing an understanding of, and being supportive of, pupils who may have very different religious beliefs from their own, different cultural practices or whose family context may challenge ideas of 'normality'. Therefore, teachers have to build their knowledge of different cultures and religions, of the changing composition of the family and trends in contemporary society. This process will often require teachers to question their own 'unquestioned beliefs', that is, their own assumptions, belief systems and values about the way they believe people should live their lives. As we saw in the last chapter, this may well raise some fundamental questions for the teacher in relation to their personal as well as professional values. It would be important here not to caricature the teacher as white and middle class, and suggest that teachers simply have to learn more about other cultures and religions and understand different family patterns of the pupils. As the teaching profession has – albeit slowly – become more diverse, teachers are faced with challenges to their own culture, religious or political beliefs, and lifestyle. This is a complex area which we can illustrate by a number of critical incidents encountered by teachers in their classrooms (see Table 7.1).

Each of the incidents in Table 7.1 raises fundamental questions for the teacher. The tensions are partly created by the competing rights of two parties or by differing perceptions, and the teacher has to find a resolution to these in order that the classroom can be genuinely inclusive. However, this is not an easy process as each incident raises a range of questions. We can explore each incident further to illustrate this.

Table 7.1 ■ Critical incidents

1	A parent makes a complaint because the teacher had recommended a fictional fantasy to one of the pupils. The pupil is interested in fantasy writing and wanted to read more for the portfolio assessment. The parent sees the book as an affront to the family's religious beliefs.
2	As a particular passage text is being studied in the class, a pupil uses this to make a sexist remark about the teacher's personal apearance.
3	The teacher questions a pupil about the signature on the permission slip for a forthcoming trip. The form has not been signed by the pupil's mother whom the teacher knows but by another adult as carer.
4	A teacher has planned a trip to the theatre. The play relates to a unit of work being read by the class but it is only being performed for two nights. When booking the tickets the teacher had not realized it clashed with a religious festival that will involve a small group of four pupils. The group has come to say that they feel excluded from this activity.
5	The teacher begins a new project to try and interest the large group of boys who are reluctant to participate in the work of the class. A group of girls object to this subject matter claiming they are fed up having to do 'boys' topics'.
6	A parent objects to the teacher's use of the term 'parent or carer' in class the previous day asserting that 'we're not all social work cases here!'

Incident 1 This is similar to the scenarios we examined in the previous chapter and raises questions about the scope of the teacher's ability to make choices. The teacher regarded the recommended text as ideal for illustrating good fantasy writing for this age group and encouraging the pupil. The text is well known to question religious belief. Which set of beliefs and values should take precedence?

Incident 2 Teachers have a duty to challenge discriminatory behaviour and language, but what do they do when they themselves are being targeted? How does the teacher keep a focus on the issue of the unacceptability of discriminatory language without it ultimately affecting her relationship with this pupil. Should this remark be put down to adolescent bravado? Would challenging this behaviour affect the relationship between the teacher and the pupil? How should a teacher be protected from the discriminatory behaviour of pupils? What might be the cost of not challenging discriminatory behaviour?

Incident 3 Given the media pressure in relation to health and safety on school trips, the teacher's questioning of the signature might be understandable. However, this incident does raise questions about issues of

confidentiality – how far should individual teachers be party to information about the family background and lifestyle of the pupil to appreciate
any difficulties the pupil might be experiencing? How far does the sharing
of such information breech confidentiality?

Incident 4 The teacher sees the play as an excellent educational opportunity for the pupils particularly the experience of seeing the play on
stage. Should some pupils be allowed to access this experience while
others cannot? Are some pupils being advantaged over others because
of their background?

Incident 5 The boys in the class have been significantly underachieving
and this is having a negative effect on attainment and the school's overall
performance. The girls tended to achieve well no matter what topics are
covered. However, it takes a considerable amount of work to motivate the
boys and so there is a need to adopt strategies that will engage them in
their own learning. However, should the needs and interests of one group
of pupils dominate? When there is pressure on schools to succeed, and
limited resourcing available, whose learning needs take priority?

Incident 6 The teacher was unaware that there were any pupils in the class
living with carers but was following the essence of the school policy on the
use of inclusive language. How far should school policies appreciate the
stance and viewpoints of others, and how far should the school and teachers make clear the set of values they stand for? What should the response
be to the parent who clearly saw this as offensive?

Some of these incidents illustrate the misunderstandings that can occur
because of a lack of knowledge or insight into diverse lifestyles and religious
or cultural beliefs and values. Other incidents illustrate the impact of discriminatory behaviour and practices on pupils, teachers and parents.
Fundamental in each of these incidents is the question of differences in
values and competing rights. Teachers need to be able to articulate their own
values not just in terms of education, but also their personal values, and consider how this shapes their actions and responses as they try to build a
genuinely inclusive classroom. Where there are clashes in values or limited
resources, teachers are also called upon to make hard decisions about whose
needs take priority in a specific circumstance in order that barriers to learning can be removed.

Diversity of learning and support needs

We now turn to the issue of addressing diverse learning and support needs in an inclusive classroom. There is no doubt that diversity in terms of learning and support needs without full resourcing has put pressure on staff and pupils alike. This has been regularly criticized – most notably by Baroness Warnock (2005) the chair of the report, *Special Educational Needs* (CEE-HCYP, 1978), which raised the question of segregated education. Baroness Warnock is now calling for a radical review in order that the children with severe learning needs can access education. However, that is not to abandon the idea of inclusive education completely as teachers will continue to work with pupils with diverse learning and support needs, and will need the appropriate knowledge and skill to undertake this task. In some ways, though, the acquisition of new knowledge and skill is the easier area in terms of teacher development. What is more important is the impact of the teacher's attitudes and expectations about the abilities of pupils on learning and achievement. In a recent study by Ainscow et al. (2003) of inclusive practices in school, the expectations of the teachers were identified as the significant barrier to pupil learning:

> What we regard as our most important finding is the extent to which barriers arise when teachers' understandings simplify the complexity of the situations in which they practise and, particularly, of the students they teach. This tends to be thrown into relief particularly at the points where established understandings are set alongside understandings derived from a different perspective; for instance: when a Canterbury researcher works with a girl with 'severe language delay', he finds that she can do far more than her teachers believe; when the teachers in one of the schools in the Newcastle study hand over their classes to an advisory teacher, they find she achieves things with them they thought impossible; and, when teachers in one of the Manchester schools hear what children have to say about their own and others' abilities, they have to rethink their notion of 'high ability'. In each of these examples, it is evident that the teachers' initial understandings have missed some of the complexity of the situation and, specifically, some of the human complexity of the students involved. The practices which we saw following from these misunderstandings – inappropriately low demands on students, teaching which focuses on what children do badly while ignoring what they do well, selection for 'ability' groups on the basis of uni-dimensional notions of ability – likewise miss this complexity and thereby create barriers for learners. (Ainscow et al., 2003: 15)

As Ainscow et al. argue, though, there is a tension that exists in education policy across the UK between the drive for improvement in pupil attainment and the pressure for developing genuinely inclusive practices in the classroom. They found that the attainment agenda has dominated the work of many teachers and limited the development of inclusive practices. In order to develop genuinely inclusive education and remove barriers to learning, teachers must:

- articulate their values
- appreciate the influence of the contexts in which they work and the interaction between these contexts – the classroom, the classroom in the school and the school within a local community and within the policy environment
- develop knowledge and understanding of the capabilities of each child within the class
- acquire skill in designing and delivering appropriate learning contexts and tasks for individuals and groups.

The political ambition for social inclusion is only one policy agenda that is shaping classroom life. There are other social tends which are reshaping the relationship between teacher and pupil, and which are of significance as we consider the teacher's professional position.

■ The classroom in a democratic society

Concerns about the disengagement of specific sectors of society from the democratic process and questions about the diminution of 'social capital', that is, the processes of trust and interactions between members of a society, have led to the placing of citizenship as an area of concern within the school. Here the ethos, organization and activities should foster pupils' interest and willingness to participate in democratic society. At school level there are examples of pupils' councils and different interest groups being set up related to specific initiatives such as the 'health-promoting school' or 'eco-schools'. The eco-school programme is a useful example of this approach:

> The scheme is rooted in a genuine desire to help children become more effective citizens by encouraging them to take responsibility for the future of their own environment ... Pupil involvement is a key part of the Eco-Schools programme. Having pupils engaged in the whole process, including monitoring, action planning and decision-making, leads to

genuine ownership of the programme and an increase in their sense of responsibility for the school environment and local area. (Eco-schools, n.d.)

Eco-schools and eco-groups are one example of fostering pupil participation. However, if such practices are confined to extra-curricular or additional activities these will have a limited impact on the pupils' understanding of genuine participation in society and the development of their own agency as citizens and learners. To be able to prepare children and young people for their future roles within a democratic society, they must be able to do more that just 'experience' democratic processes in narrowly defined areas of activity but, instead, be part of the processes of decision-making in core areas of school and classroom life, that is, learning. In the previous chapter we considered the changing school context with the move to flatter structures that would encourage distributed leadership and collaborative practice between teachers. These processes of participation and open decision-making are equally relevant when we consider the role of the pupil in the classroom in a democratic society. Therefore, citizenship in schools and classrooms has to represent more than tokenistic gestures, and mark a genuine move away from the traditional power relationships, in order that the classroom becomes a context for discussion and negotiation about core issues, particularly pupil learning. Apple and Beane (1999) define what they see as a democratic school:

> in a democratic school it is true that all of those directly involved in the school, including young people, have the right to participate in the process of decision making. For this reason, democratic schools are marked by widespread participation in issues of governance and policy making. Committees, councils and other school wide decision-making groups include not only professional educators, but also young people, their parents and other members of the school community. In classrooms, young people and teachers engage in collaborative planning, reaching decisions that respond to the concerns, aspirations and interests of both. This kind of democratic planning at both school and the classroom levels, is not 'engineering of consent' towards predetermined decisions that has too often created the illusion of democracy, but a genuine attempt to honour the right of people to participate in making decisions that affect their lives. (Apple and Beane, 1999: 10)

However, the pressure to genuinely engage learners in their own learning is not just coming from concerns about the future development of democratic society but from other legislative frameworks and policies.

■ The changing position of the learner

Up until this point we have very much focused on the role of the teacher within an inclusive classroom. There have been a number of different developments both in terms of social policy and legislation that is changing the position of the learner. In the traditional classroom setting the roles of teacher and pupil were strictly divided – you were either a teacher or a learner – and implicit in this was an unequal power relationship. The role of the pupils was passive: they were to be taught by the teacher and to learn quietly and obediently. This was the dominant image characterizing the legal as well as social position of children. Children did not have legal rights. Instead, parents held these rights and responsibilities, and leave was given to teachers to act *in loco parentis*. Article 12 of the United Nation's (UNCHR, 1991) *Convention on the Rights of the Child* states that children have a right to be involved in decisions that will affect them. Though this may refer to family matters, there is a principle here that is applicable to the child or young person's role in relation to her/his own learning. Now the dominant ideologies as well as legal and policy frameworks foreground the active participation of the child or young person. Further, both as a matter of social justice and economic development, policies on lifelong learning have been developed. These do not begin in post-school education and training, but represent principles to be nurtured from the early years of a learner's career. The agency of the learner becomes a central issue to enable pupils to become self-directive and autonomous learners.

These wider social influences are shaping the daily life in classrooms in the UK, where new demands made on teachers fundamentally alter the power relationships between the teacher and the pupil. The processes start from the early stages of school where there is an emphasis on learners learning together, learners taking responsibility for their own learning and behaviour both individually and collectively and learners party to the determination of their learning programme, and these practices should continue throughout their progress as a lifelong learner. We can see these trends in the following:

- the development of approaches such as co-operative and collaborative learning among learners – the group of learners becomes an equally important context for learning as the interaction between teacher and pupils
- the use of strategies such as peer tutoring and peer mediation – pupils take responsibility for the learning and behaviour of their fellow pupils
- development of personalized learning – learning plans have to be agreed between learner, parents and teachers.

Such developments in the learning processes of the classroom reshape the task of the teacher (Table 7.2).

Table 7.2 ■ Creating the autonomous learner: the tasks of the teacher

Consult with learners

Listen to the views of learners

Enable learners to make decisions about their own learning

Create contexts in which learners can make decisions

Enable pupils to develop skills of learning

Establish contexts to enable learners to learn constructively from each other

These developments also raise questions about teachers' understanding and skill in relation to the learning process. We now turn to the question of teachers learning about learning.

■ Learning about learning

There has been a significant expansion of our theoretical understanding of learning processes. This has helped to assert the centrality of learning in classroom life. A wide and varied range of research and theoretical work has moved our understanding of learning beyond conceptualizations which see learning as a process associated with a fixed notion of a general intelligence, to looking at the cognitive, social and emotional dimensions of learning. The work of, among others, popular writers such as Gardner (1984) on multiple intelligence, Goleman (1996) on emotional intelligence and Jensen (1995) on the functioning of the brain and learning have been taken up within education. Where traditionally there has been a gap between the work of theorists and the application of these ideas in the classroom, currently what is noteworthy is that the expansion in knowledge in the field of learning has been accompanied by a significant growth in teachers' interest in learning itself. Partly this is due to the development of programmes such as co-operative learning, critical skills, assertive discipline and assessment as a part of learning. Each of these provides set strategies and techniques that enable teachers to extend their repertoire. There is no doubt that such programmes are having an impact on the practice and understanding of individual teachers. Hallam et al. (2004) reporting on the implementation of the Assessment is for Learning programme in Scottish schools illustrate well this impact on the development of teachers:

One of the most positive outcomes of the project was the overwhelming enthusiasm and commitment demonstrated by teachers ... They are now better informed, have engaged with the literature and developed their thinking. They have considered their practice critically, worked through the ideas personally, found creative solutions and shared their ideas with others. They reported deeper understanding of the learning process and what involving pupils in their own learning actually meant. There have been major changes in their attitudes and they now believe that they can improve the quality of learning in their classrooms for their pupils and for themselves. There have been changes in the power relationships in the classroom with them being more prepared to relax control and empower their pupils.

The project Assessment is for Learning has very much centred upon enabling teachers and schools to develop and reflect on practice. This and other developments in teaching and learning are having a significant impact on teachers' development and work in a number of different ways, including their:

- understanding of the teaching and learning processes
- pedagogic practice in the classroom
- understanding of the role of the pupils in their own learning
- attitudes towards their own development as teachers.

■ The e-classroom

We have argued that educational policies related to inclusion and to lifelong learning are part of a wider political vision about the sustaining and enhancement of a prosperous and participatory democratic society. The realization of these policies has to be principally undertaken within the classroom. Resourcing currently is helping to reshape the context of the classroom and the role of the teacher. First, there is the ongoing investment in information and communications technology (ICT) and, secondly, there is the investment in not only additional teaching staff but also para-professionals whose task is to support the learning of pupils.

As we develop both our understanding and strategies for e-learning, the possibilities and practical applications of ICT are extending. With the increasing pace of these developments, a range of powerful technologies will be readily available which allow pupils to access knowledge, to develop skills and to interact in different forums and contexts without the immediate direction or presence of a teacher. We need a new understanding of the pedagogies appropriate for a twenty-first century education system. Initially the emphasis in policy and development was on building teacher's understanding of ICT but this is changing: '[t]he move has shifted somewhat from learning *about* ICT to learning *with* the support of or *through* ICT' (SEED, 2005b: 8 original emphasis). The policy direction is clear:

> Traditional methods have not achieved enough. The wider availability of new technology means that we have both the opportunity – and the responsibility – to explore new approaches to teaching and learning. The familiar and effective teaching methods of listening, reading, writing and class discussion will of course remain important. But our teaching institutions ought to be advancing beyond the traditional formats that are still so prevalent. (SEED, 2005b: 27)

This standpoint is echoed in the policy on technology and learning within the English educational system, *Harnessing Technology: Transforming Learning and Children's Services* (DfES, 2005a), which sets out three areas for development:

- the quantity and range of resources available to teachers and learners
- the quality and degree of innovation of those resources
- the embedding of e-learning and the curriculum (DfES, 2005a: 28).

This emphasis on the use of ICT to improve learning is reconstructing the classroom and the role of the teacher within educational policy documents. The following extract from a briefing paper for the Empowering Schools in Northern Ireland strategy (DENI, 2004b) provides an interesting illustration of the way in which the classroom and the role of the teacher are being reconstructed in the policy imagination:

> Eddy has arrived at school. As he enters the door his pupil number is scanned, the form register database is updated and he goes straight to the open learning area. He logs on to retrieve yesterday's homework, marked ready for today's English lesson, and checks his mark register. Last night, he completed two homework assignments on a tablet PC and stored these in his user area on the school network: one has been computer-marked already.

> ... Mrs Green starts with a lesson she prepared the previous week. She is able to access all the resources from home and was able to get the latest CCEA template, exemplar lesson plans and other materials on Learning NI, the online environment for Northern Ireland ... Based on information

on each child from the LNI assessment and progress report module she arranged her class into three ability groups, each of which has its own learning pathway for this topic. Eddy is doing well at the minute. He opens his saved homework file and his results spreadsheet appears on all the other computer screens for the class to see and discuss. Mrs Green is pleased to be able to confirm his move to the top group. His learning pathway includes a review of two short videos, an interactive simulation on sequencing, some digital pictures, a simple test, and an investigational activity in the NASA Internet site.

During lunch, the open-plan areas are full of pupils. One group discusses a forthcoming multimedia presentation, they are delighted that a key member of the group who has been ill is going to make her contribution from home by videoconference. Two of the group are nervous, they have completed a module and take their final assessments on-line today.

After school, Eddy has basketball practice. Eddy's basketball is monitored by axions – sensors that monitor the pressure on the ball, and his trajectory and velocity across the hall before he makes a shot. During a break, his video glasses show him professionals making similar shots and suggests some practice drills to improve performance. (DENI, 2004b: 1–2).

In this extract there is a real sense of a motivated and skilled learner, but the teacher's role has also altered. The teacher, traditionally, has been positioned as the lynchpin of the social processes that support learning in the context of the classroom. In this projection a central task of the teacher is the construction of learning pathways: the teacher provides the context, the programme and the resources for the pupils to use to follow their personal learning plan. This vision differs substantially from pedagogic practices where the teacher is very much the centre of the interactional processes in the delivery of the curriculum.

The other area where there has been substantial resourcing from government has been the introduction of para-professionals in the classroom and this development also repositions the teacher as the designer and manager of the learning context, rather than solely a deliverer of the curriculum.

■ Para-professionals in the classroom

Historically, the classroom and the teaching and learning process has been the sole locus of the teacher but there now is a more complex understanding of the learning process and a blurring of these lines: for pupils to achieve their potential, a range of participants is involved. Support staff have long had a role in schools, particularly as 'auxiliaries' releasing teachers from playground or dinner duty or from administrative tasks or from the preparation and organization of resources (Clayton, 1993). However, more recently this role has expanded and now, as part of the staff of a school, there are classroom assistants who support the learning of children. Wilson et al. (2003) in an evaluation of the use of classroom assistants report that:

> Classroom assistants help pupils stay on task and achieve more while the teacher is working with others, and they provide reinforcement through games and activities. They also enable teachers to offer a wide range of practical and interactive learning experiences, by supervising groups of pupils engaged in such tasks. Many respondents [teachers] believed that classroom assistants were contributing to improvements in pupils' motivation, confidence and self-esteem. (Wilson et al., 2003: 203)

And these findings echo the findings of studies of the use of learning support assistants in English schools (Woolfson and Truswell, 2005). One of the significant issues emerging from the range of studies has been the relationship between the teacher and the classroom assistant. With a classroom assistant in the classroom interacting with pupils, the teacher's role now includes one of leadership and supervision of the classroom assistant – people management roles that have been played in the past by those in management posts in the school. There is also a more fundamental question this raises which is the relative professional standing of a teacher and a classroom assistant. Muijs and Reynolds (2003) highlight the current limited entry requirements and training of classroom assistants. The demarcation between teacher and classroom assistant is something that has been clearly asserted by the GTC in Scotland: 'The General Teaching Council for Scotland has always believed that the role of the classroom assistant needed to be carefully defined to ensure that there is no confusion between the tasks a teacher should undertake and tasks a classroom assistant should undertake' (GTCS, 2003b: 6).

In England there has been the introduction of 'high level teaching assistants' but again a clear line is drawn between the role of a qualified teacher and an assistant's role: 'teachers and high level teaching assistants are not interchangeable and this principle will be reflected in new regulations to be introduced under section 133 of the Education Act 2002' (DfES, 2002: 13).

Though the roles of classroom assistants and teachers are not interchangeable, nevertheless the development of para-professionalism within education has influenced the evolution of the role of the teacher. At the same time the role of the teacher, as we have seen, is being reshaped by a range of influences: societal change, the impact of technology and research on the process of education.

To this point, we have looked across a range of policy documents from the different systems in the UK and traced some of the developments in relation to the changing role and position of the teacher. In the previous chapter we looked at the idea of 'distributed leadership' within the context of the school. Here we want to consider this notion of teacher leadership within the classroom context. Underpinning the concept of 'teacher leadership' is the idea of a person who shapes and manages the learning context (whether this is within the classroom, beyond the classroom, or in a virtual learning environment), and who leads the activities of others, (para-professionals, professionals and pupils) in order to secure effective learning.

■ Teacher leadership

Crowther and Olsen (1997) from their study of individuals who were perceived not only as excellent classroom practitioners but also noted for their ability to stimulate and influence change, identified a number of characteristics. An underpinning assumption was that of excellence in pedagogic practice and, in addition to this, the authors propose the following framework for teachers as leaders. They can:

- articulate clear views of a better world
- model trust and sincerity
- build networks of support
- nurture a culture of success (Crowther and Olsen, 1997: 11).

Crowther and Olsen's study focused on teacher leaders who would work within areas of social and economic disadvantage and one of the significant themes was the sense of advocacy. (Importantly also, given the previous discussion, two of the sample of 15 were para-professionals demonstrating how boundaries are constantly being challenged.) In these characteristics there is a strong sense of improvement – not in managerial terms of improvement in examination results and other indicators reflecting narrowly based evidence, but more in terms of a change orientation to improve the conditions of learning and opportunity on a wider social front. Crowther and Olsen (1997) emphasize this values orientation and the centrality of excellence in teaching to support pupils' learning for their long-term growth, development and opportunity:

> Teacher leadership is essentially an ethical stance that is based on views of both a better world and the power of teaching to shape meaning systems. It manifests itself in actions that involve the wider community and leads to the creation of new forms of understanding that will enhance the quality of life in the community in the long term. It reaches its potential in contexts where system and school structures are facilitative and appreciative. (Crowther and Olsen, 1997: 12)

In the previous chapter we considered some of the organizational issues that would support the development of distributed or teacher leadership. However, there are other factors that Frost and Harris (2003) identify as related to what they term 'personal capacities':

- authority – based on the understanding and skills of the teacher who can demonstrate excellent classroom practice
- knowledge (pedagogical, organizational, community) – an understanding of teaching processes, of how the specific school works, of wider community needs and contexts
- situational understanding – the ability to read and understand situations and anticipate the reactions of others
- interpersonal skills – being able to interact, communicate and influence others.

■ Conclusion

In the changing context of the classroom, development of teachers then is not simply about raising teachers' awareness about new areas of knowledge or to acquire skill in the use of a defined set of pedagogic practices. There are attitudinal as well as philosophical considerations as teachers grapple with the daily reality of these policies. In addition to this, as Harris and Frost (2003) argue, the evolution of teacher leadership will demand enhanced personal skills as well as significant changes in behaviour on the part of the teacher. Coolahan (2002), looking at the development of teachers, argues that

> It is only intelligent, highly skilled, imaginative, caring and well educated teachers who will be able to respond satisfactorily to the demands placed on the education system in developed societies. If society's concern is to improve quality in education and to foster creative, enterprising, innovative, self reliant young people, with the capacity and motivation to

go on as lifelong learners, then this will not happen unless the corps of teachers are themselves challenging, innovative and lifelong learners. The future well-being of the teaching profession in the context of a lifelong learning policy framework is of pivotal importance. It is necessary to view the career of teaching nowadays in a systemic way which locates it within the role required of it by a fast changing society and school environment. (Coolahan, 2002: 12–13)

The challenge then is similar to that posed in previous chapters – how we enable teachers to face these new demands where teachers' traditional authority and professional role are being reconstructed to facilitate the influence of the pupil and also the parent voice to shape and contribute to the teaching and learning process.

SECTION C

PROFESSIONAL DEVELOPMENT

8 Teacher professional development and progression for the twenty-first century

Chapter outline

This chapter explores changes in professional development for teachers and the new career pathways and opportunities that have become available in recent years. In the previous chapter we showed the position of teachers in relation to their responsibility of leading learning. In this chapter we consider the role of continuing professional development in helping teachers adapt to and become equipped for the new roles required of them and compare the new models for professional development and progression that now exist in the UK.

Keywords

■ Continuing professional development

■ Performance threshold

■ Advanced Skills Teacher

■ Chartered Teacher

■ Excellent Teacher

■ Teachers in the twenty-first century

In the previous chapter we looked at the organizational context of the school and the implications of this for teacher identity and development. The school, though, as we indicated, is part of a larger educational system in which teacher policy is of central importance.

A key policy feature in education in the early years of the twenty-first century has been the negotiation and agreement of new conditions of service and pay for teachers. This is described variously as remodelling or restructuring and outlined in documents such as *A Teaching Profession for the 21st Century* (Scotland: SEED, 2001a), and *Raising Standards and Tackling Workload: A National Agreement* (England and Wales: DfES, 2003). In Northern Ireland (NI), the Committee of Inquiry on Teachers' Pay and Conditions of Service, delivered the second and final part of its report in February 2004, entitled *Improving Conditions, Raising Standards and Negotiating Arrangements* (DENI, 2004a). Such developments are not unique to the UK. Similar initiatives in Australia in 2000 resulted in *Teachers for the 21st Century: Making the Difference* (DEST, 2000). It is important, then, not to view these developments in isolation but as part of reform of the teaching profession that is also shaped by the school improvement agenda and the discourse of the 'new professional'.

There are a numbers of drivers for such agreements, but the reference to the twenty-first century in the Australian document (leaving aside millennium mania) implies that in the new age, the role of teachers will be qualitatively very different. In our previous chapters we have shown that the context in which teachers operate has changed radically and rapidly in the past 30 years. The decline of traditional industries, the rise of a knowledge- and technology-based economy, government policies of wider access to third-level education and lifelong learning, changing work patterns and societal changes, particularly to family structures, have all impacted on teachers and their classroom practice. Teachers have had to try both to accommodate these changes and adapt to this rapidly changing environment. It would be true to say that they have not been fully supported professionally in doing this, nor has the profession itself evolved and adapted to reflect this altered environment.

Teacher professionalism has become increasingly politicized. There are many reasons for this and some have been referred to already, such as the implications of socio-economic change, nationally and globally. Clearly, the school improvement agenda, based on economic, social and political imperatives, has been a driving force, with teachers viewed alternatively as contributors to the schools' standards crisis and as the agents for effecting change. In an age of performance management, a predominant view is that there is a causal link between educational underachievement and the quality of teaching and learning experienced in the classroom. The effect of this is to link educational success more closely to teacher performance and to heighten society's awareness and expectations of teachers. In many respects this contributed to the professional malaise that set in in the 1980s and 1990s, creating greater disaffection within the teaching profession.

In England and Wales, much of this disaffection stemmed from the changes introduced by the Education Reform Act 1988. Menter et al. (2006: 2) caution that 'The lasting impact of those five years should not be underestimated. Teachers' trust of politicians and civil servants was seriously undermined, which may partially account for the extremely cynical responses from which later policy initiatives were to receive from primary teachers'. This was manifest in a 'discourse of derision', discussed earlier, to which teachers were subjected by politicians in order to cover policy weaknesses, and this was actively promoted and reproduced in the mass media, often not without sensation.

Recruitment and retention are also powerful drivers of the professional development agenda. With an ageing teaching workforce (50 per cent of teachers in England are over 45) and with large numbers of teachers due to retire in the course of the next 15 years, there is a need to ensure that there are sufficient experienced teachers while providing opportunities for teachers to develop professionally. The worrying statistic that fewer than 50 per cent of teachers who begin teacher training in England remain in teaching after five years, causes concerns regarding teacher numbers but also raises questions about the development opportunities and level of support available to these early career professionals (House of Commons, Education and Skills Committee, 2004: 8).

New agreements on teachers' terms and conditions of service, reflect what is evident to most teachers in their classrooms – that the role of the classroom practitioner has changed greatly in recent decades. This chalkface reality is articulated well by one teacher in a posting in a *Times Educational Supplement* (TES) chat room: 'Naively I thought teaching was going to be about teaching. Well now I realise that on top of that we have to act as: policeman, bouncer, councillor, administrator, psychologist, social worker, role model, Butlins redcoat' (*TES* Online Forum, 2005b).

In the twenty-first century a teacher is an active professional, liaising and collaborating with a number of other professionals, managing not only learning and teaching in their own classrooms, but also managing other staff such as para-professionals, while engaging in ongoing professional development, with a growing expectation that this will be accredited by an official body.

A key feature of this remodelling/restructuring of the teaching profession has been the central role assigned to the professional development of teachers, extending the concept from in-service training (INSET) to continuing professional development (CPD). In earlier chapters we asked our central question – can teachers forge new professional identities which will help them to claim or reclaim ownership of their profession? (Chapter 1) – and speculated that one desirable way to achieve this is through professional development, reflection and enquiry (Chapter 5). We suggested that reflective practice can be a powerful tool and resource for changing practice, where it is used appropriately, from a critical standpoint, and as part of a structured and supported programme or initiative. We have suggested that teachers are not isolated professionals but are part of a professional learning community, with a collective task of supporting, developing and enhancing the learning experiences of pupils, and we showed how organizational contexts impact upon professional identity and autonomy.

Our premise is that the changed and changing learning and teaching environment requires teachers to work in new and different ways, and with a wider range of other professionals and para-professionals. This puts greater emphasis on the development of teachers and on CPD; and it is this changing CPD landscape and the new development, progression and career opportunities now available to teachers that form the focus of this chapter.

■ Continuing professional development

With new developments in CPD for teachers in the UK in recent years, it is now possible to say that there is a CPD continuum or framework for professional development, which enables teachers to progress on a career pathway and to be remunerated for it. In England and Wales the career pathway for classroom practitioners (as distinct from that for those wishing to take up management responsibility) has five main levels (Table 8.1), while in Scotland an eight-level model (Table 8.2) of professional development has evolved. In both cases, these represent a new 'cradle to grave' model of teacher progression and development.

Table 8.1 ■ Teachers' career pathways in England and Wales

Newly qualified teacher (NQT)

Classroom teacher

Performance threshold

Advanced skills teacher

Excellent teacher

Table 8.2 ■ Scotland's eight-level model of professional development

	Career stage	Standard	Academic qualification
1	Probationer Teacher	Standard for Full Registration	Initial Teacher Education Qualification
2	Fully Registered Teacher		
3	Experienced Teacher		
4	Experienced Teacher aspiring to Chartered Teacher	Standard for Chartered Teacher	Master's Degree
5	Chartered Teacher		
6	Educational Leaders	Aspects of Standard for Headship	
7	Educational Leaders aspiring to Headship	Standard for Headship	PgDip in School Leadership and Management (SQH)
8	Head teachers		

Source: Based on 'Eight stages of excellence' outlined by Scotland's National CPD Co-ordinator, Margaret Alcorn, in *Times Educational Supplement*, Scotland, 6 May 2005.

Recognition that CPD has a role to play in raising standards and enhancing professionalism opens the discussion as to what actually constitutes CPD and how teachers can engage with it. In *Leading and Managing Continuing Professional Development*, Earley and Bubb (2004), cite Tomlinson's observation that

> The first national enquiry into in-service education training was not mounted until 1970, which seems to suggest that it had been broadly assumed that initial education and training would suffice for a professional lifetime. It is an assumption rooted in a view, perhaps held subconsciously rather than formalized as policy, that the task of the teacher remained constant. (Tomlinson, 1993, in Earley and Bubb, 2004: 6)

In the 30 or more years since the first national enquiry, policies to formalize CPD have been developed and documented as strategies for CPD. In England, a national CPD strategy was launched in March 2001 (DfEE, 2001c), with CPD co-ordinators now appointed at local authority, school and, in Scotland, at national level, to oversee implementation.

In Scotland it was recognized that CPD provision and delivery needed to be more coherent, structured and regulated. A consultation document issued by the Scottish Office in 1998 noted: 'beyond initial teacher education there are no statements of additional competences and standards to inform development, no overall framework to give coherence to teachers' development, and no structure of qualifications to work towards that gives recognition to teachers' increased remits and professional skills' (SOEID, 1998: 1). In Scotland subsequent changes have been brought about through *A Teaching Profession for the 21st Century* (the McCrone Agreement; SEED, 2001a), leading to a radically altered career pathway for classroom practitioners, linked to their engagement with CPD.

Another aspect of this changing CPD landscape is the role given to existing or recently formed General Teaching Councils. In Scotland, the remit of the oldest teaching council in the UK, the GTCS, was extended by Act of Parliament to include career development (Standards in Scotland's Schools Act 2000, Section 45, item 2). When the General Teaching Council in Northern Ireland was established in 2004, one of it is first acts was to initiate a consultation on CPD, resulting in the publication of the *Code of Practice and Professional Standards* (GTCNI, 2004). In England, the role of the General Teaching Council in career development is less explicit and less extensive, explained in large part by the existence of the Teacher Training Agency (TTA and, from 2005, the Training and Development Agency for Schools), which has been and continues to be the strategic locus for teacher professional development in England. Nevertheless it is possible to say that in recent years a more coherent, structured and co-ordinated approach to CPD is evolving within each education system in the UK, evident in the models for development, progression and career advancement that have emerged

Teacher professional development: CPD and new career pathways

A central element of the reform of the teaching profession is the requirement of teachers to engage in professional development activities for a specified period. Since 1 September 2005 all teachers in England have had an entitlement to a guaranteed minimum of 10 per cent of their timetabled teaching commitment for planning, preparation and assessment (PPA). This is linked to CPD in that the purpose of PPA is to 'enable teachers to raise standards through individual or collaborative professional activity' (National Remodelling Team, 2003).

In Scotland teachers are committed to undertake 35 hours of CPD each year. This requires them to engage in a variety of developmental activities as part of their contractual obligations. These activities are usually reached in agreement with a line manager, form part of the teacher's personal development review (PRD) and are often recorded in a CPD portfolio. There can be wide variety in the sort of activities teachers engage with as part of this mandatory CPD. For some, the school closely prescribes this; for others it is self-determined. Consequently, while one teacher might undertake an accredited (award-bearing) programme of study, another might view reading an educational newspaper or journal on a weekly basis as constituting their CPD.

There are a number of explanations for the introduction of mandatory CPD. Traditional INSET courses were often seen as unsatisfactory, with limited impact on classroom practice. Such courses were usually short day-courses provided either in school, by the local education authority (LEA) or by external providers such as external consultants or higher education institutions (HEIs) and were often specifically related to curriculum content. Further, attendance at these courses was, with the exception of courses provided to cover national developments, entirely voluntary in nature and often no profile of attendance or outcomes for the individual was kept. Variations in the quality of CPD experiences and opportunities provided by these frequently had a negative effect on teachers. The proliferation of the number of educational consultants, especially in the 1990s, made possible by the opening up of a largely unregulated CPD market, contributed to this. This, indeed, could be seen as the high point of 'guru-led' CPD.

Part of the reason for the dissatisfaction with CPD provision and delivery was its 'one-off' nature and there were few opportunities to develop this in a sustained way over time. The Scottish CPD consultation document also recognized that 'While we have established some courses for CPD, which are well supported by teachers, the arrangements for CPD are not generally systematic or well directed' (SOEID 1998: 3).

It was recognized that CPD provision and delivery needed to be more coherent, structured and regulated. In Scotland the creation of a National

Part of the difficulty is the way threshold has been presented and understood. One way of viewing it is as a means of managing a pay rise, without making the rise uniformly applicable. Certainly, some teachers seem to equate it with this. Menter et al. cite one teacher from their survey who responded 'I just don't think it's fair that we actually have to apply for our own pay rise' (2006: 5) Among some teachers, there is a prevailing culture where career advancement and salary remuneration are seen as automatic, whereas in other comparable professions this has not been the case for many years.

Teachers also seem to perceive the process as having little impact on practice and view it as an unnecessary form-filling exercise. This, however, is very much a matter of interpretation and expectation. Menter et al. argue that 'if practice is interpreted as referring more broadly to wider aspects of teachers' work, then threshold has a marked impact' (2006: 8).

On another level, however, threshold can be viewed as career enhancing. The process of reflecting on performance, of demonstrating how practice meets threshold standards, and selecting and providing evidence to support this, can be both affirmative and developmental, particularly when the outcome is successful. It may also highlight future areas for CPD activity. Of our three CPD measurements, threshold only meets one – reviewing practice – but that is not to devalue its role and contribution. Threshold may be limited in what it can offer teachers in terms of professional development, but its crucial role might be in setting teachers on a developmental pathway, which takes them to the next stage and beyond.

Advanced Skills Teachers

The post of AST was introduced in England and Wales in 1998 (ASTs have not been introduced in Northern Ireland) and was presented as part of a package of initiatives designed to provide 'more career progression opportunities for the best teachers'. In addition to AST, this package included performance threshold and the fast-track initiative. The need specifically for AST posts was to 'recognize and retain the best teachers' (DfES, 2001a).

Beyond the published reasons for the creation of ASTs, it is possible to discern other factors influencing the introduction of this new post. We have discussed previously the urgency of the issue of retention, both in terms of early career professionals and more experienced teachers. In addition, the dominance of the school improvement agenda, effected through performance management, has put the spotlight on the classroom practitioner.

Previously, the only opportunity for classroom practitioners to achieve career promotion, and the accompanying benefits and status, was to pursue a management role. Once in position, the influence of these highly competent classroom practitioners on learning and teaching was less immediate and direct. As we argued in Chapter 7, the establishment of line management systems in schools in the late 1980s and 1990s as the conduit for implementation of national policy resulted in a division between the management and teaching, separating managers from the core business of any school, the teaching and learning processes, and separating teachers from the processes of decision-making about teaching and learning in the school. Thus a reason for the creation of ASTs is to disseminate expertise into learning and teaching that previously was channelled into management.

Further, it could also be argued that, given New Labour's emphasis on education as a central pivot of policy, a rapid response to the schools' crisis, with immediate effects was desirable and ASTs are one way to achieve this. This links to a commonly held assumption that the best teachers, often those who undertook further study and engaged more widely with CPD, would seek career advancement through a management position, as the only form of career progression available to them. This meant that classroom practitioners, many highly competent and highly expert, nonetheless were perceived as needing to develop their skills and knowledge, and in the worst cases, were viewed as the 'rump' of the profession. In the 1980s and 1990s, this was evident in a downwards spiral of declining morale and a devaluing of the classroom practitioner but it is a view that persists. In March 2005, in a special feature, the *Times Educational Supplement* described the outreach role of the AST 'superteacher' as 'fighting the evils of sloppy practice and spreading good advice and exemplar material' (Hastings, 2005).

Another argument is that AST represents the traditional cascading of CPD in a new format and, in a climate of performativity, a cheaper but potentially more efficient and effective option than providing specific CPD opportunities for all teachers. In many respects the creation of AST addresses these needs in three ways: (1) aspirationally, as an incentive to develop professionally, (2) as a cohort of expert teachers effecting change in their own classrooms and (3) as a resource for helping other teachers develop their practice.

Unlike the Scottish Chartered Teacher which is a designation of status rather than a post, in England, a school decides whether or not to create an AST post and then advertises externally as well as internally for applicants. The post is funded by the local education authority. Applicants must demon-

In some instances ASTs undertake roles that previously would have been filled by local educational authority advisers. Pressure on resources at LEA level makes AST an attractive option for head teachers seeking support for school improvement initiatives. The ASTs can fill gaps in the LEA's provision of subject-focused and other specialized advice with the advantage that their deployment can be more widely spread. Such substitution of roles can create tension, with ASTs viewed as a potential threat by some LEA advisers. More positively, ASTs are increasingly viewed as teachers capable of working along-side advisers and complementing their work, and as a key element in LEA strategies to raise standards in teaching and learning (Taylor and Jennings, 2004: 16).

However, dissonance between how ASTs view their role and how it is viewed by head teachers and LEAs can make the outreach remit of ASTs more complex, particularly as ASTs tend to see themselves as deliverers of specialist support rather than as school improvement generalists (Taylor and Jennings, 2004: 9). With time, training and appropriate professional development this dissonance may reduce so that ASTs come to be viewed, and view themselves, as part of team for effecting change and bringing about improvement.

However, in terms of further professional development, once the grade has been achieved and an AST post secured, findings from Taylor and Jennings's research and Office for Standards in Education (OFSTED) inspections suggests that this remains unsatisfactory. This relates particularly to the outreach role. Taylor and Jennings found that more than two-thirds of the 1,000 ASTs surveyed regarded the preparation and training they had received so far for their teacher-developer role to be deficient or non-existent. Given the complexities of the tasks ASTs engage in through outreach, from supporting weak and failing teachers to leading curriculum innovations, this is a worrying deficit. Taylor and Jennings draw attention to the assumption that being an excellent teacher of pupils is a necessary and sufficient condition for working with adults. They note that 'The wide variety of work assigned to them also assumes that ASTs are as well equipped to undertake work with weak or failing teachers, as they are to deliver curriculum development projects' (Taylor and Jennings, 2004: 10).

An OFSTED report in 2003 found that 'a few ASTs were sent into schools which were in very challenging circumstances and where there were unreasonable expectations of what they could achieve' (OFSTED, 2003: 9).

In Taylor and Jennings's research, the ASTs surveyed felt that they rarely had time for reading or adequate access to appropriate literature and the researchers suggest a role for HEIs supporting ASTs more actively by providing access, disseminating research and collaborating with ASTs on research projects. A future possibility is university accreditation of outreach work (Taylor and Jennings, 2004: 10, 14).

Returning to our three-score measurement of CPD – reviewing practice, acquiring new skills and knowledge, sharing good practice and experience with colleagues and new entrants to the profession – ASTs appear to impact positively in all three areas, though the evidence shows that it is in the area of outreach that the impact is greatest. Advanced Skills Teachers are supported in acquiring new skills and knowledge through training and networks, but ASTs view the latter as more effective than the former. The process of applying to becoming an AST, involving reflecting on practice, appears also to be a positive experience, with all those interviewed by Taylor and Jennings reporting that they felt valued and were pleased that their expertise had been recognized. Taylor and Jennings conclude that 'the creation of ASTs appears, therefore, to have been successful in its objective to "recognize and retain the best teachers"' (Taylor and Jennings, 2004: 11).

Excellent Teachers

The final tier of the restructured teaching profession in England and Wales, Excellent Teacher (ET), will be in place and available to teachers from September 2006. The Excellent Teacher Scheme (ETS) is aimed at 'the very best classroom practitioners' and is seen as widening the opportunity of career advancement of such teachers beyond the AST or leadership routes (Teachernet, 2005a: 2)

The Excellent Teacher is viewed as the pinnacle of a classroom teacher's role and a distinctive part of the teaching career structure. Unlike AST, there is no outreach attached to the role and ET is viewed as a resource for other teachers, requiring length, breadth and depth of experience, pedagogic excellence, and coaching and mentoring skills of a high order (Teachernet, 2005a: 2). Like AST, ET is a post created by schools and ETs will have a clearly defined role. Many of the activities that ETs could be involved with in this role are similar to those often undertaken by ASTs as part of their outreach, for example :

- induction of newly qualified teachers
- professional mentoring of other teachers
- sharing good practice through demonstration lessons
- helping teachers to develop their expertise in planning, preparation and assessment

- helping other teachers to evaluate the impact of their learning on pupils
- undertaking classroom observations to assist and support the performance management process
- helping teachers improve their teaching practice including those on capability procedures (Teachernet, 2005a: 3).

To become an ET, a teacher must have been paid on scale U3 for not less than two years when they take up the post. If eligible, applicants must meet all six of the ETS standards (Table 8.3) – currently the same as AST. They should either be employed in a school where a vacancy for an ET exists or have been assessed already as meeting the AST standards (Teachernet, 2005a: 4–5).

Table 8.3 ■ Excellent Teacher standards

1	Excellent results/outcomes
2	Excellent subject and/or specialist knowledge
3	Excellent ability to plan
4	Excellent ability to teach, manage pupils and maintain discipline
5	Excellent ability to assess and evaluate
6	Excellent abilty to advise and support other teachers

While the preliminary documentation released from the DfES about ETS outlines the process for appointing ETs, and the role and duties associated with the post, there is no indication of how this should relate to AST, other than its representation as 'widening the opportunity of career advancement of such teachers beyond the AST or leadership routes' (Teachernet, 2005a: 2). Similarities in the process of appointment and the application of the same standards to the two posts, and conversely the omission of the outreach obligation of AST from the ET post, suggests that the success of ASTs in outreach and as part of school improvement, has necessitated an extension.

Chartered Teacher

The Scottish CPD framework and pathway for career progression differs from the English model in a variety of ways, as we have seen. As elsewhere in the UK, teachers in Scotland are obliged to undertake 35 hours of CPD. However, there is no comparable performance threshold – although Scottish teachers participate in performance review and development.

The introduction of Chartered Teacher in 2003 marked a radical new development in CPD in Scotland, providing a new career pathway, recognizing the professional development of teachers and providing financial remuneration for this. Teachers who have reached the top of the main salary scale and have maintained a CPD portfolio from 2002, are eligible to apply for admission to programmes leading to the award of Chartered Teacher. Unlike Advanced Skills Teacher, Chartered Teacher is recognition of professional status rather than a specific role and is linked to a postgraduate programme of study.

Chartered Teacher emerged as a result of a process of national consultation and negotiation with key stakeholders, resulting in the convening of a committee in 1999, chaired by Professor Gavin McCrone, to enquire into teachers' careers and conditions of service. This was preceded by or coincided with several developments, all coalescing around the issue of teacher professionalism. In 1997, the Sutherland Report had recommended the development of a national framework for CPD. How this might be developed was the focus of a national consultation on CPD, initiated by the Scottish Office (SOEID, 1998b). In 2000, the Standards in Scotland's Schools Act extended the remit of the GTCS to include professional development (Bryce and Humes, 2003: 943).

The remit of the McCrone committee was to enquire into the professional conditions of service for teachers. The impetus arose from ongoing tension with the teachers' unions regarding a pay settlement for teachers. The convening of the McCrone committee was an attempt to offset any potential industrial unrest or dispute resulting from a failure to reach agreement (Pickard and Dobie, 2003: 50). The McCrone committee reported its findings in the McCrone Report in 2000 and, after a further round of negotiations with the teachers' unions, a final agreement was reached – *A Teaching Profession for the 21st Century* (SEED, 2001a).

The McCrone Report had recommended the creation of two new grades for teachers, Chartered Teacher and Advanced Chartered Teacher (Pickard and Dobie, 2003: 51). In the final agreement, however, within the revised career structure there was to be only one grade for classroom teachers – Chartered Teacher.

Like AST, and subsequently ET, the CT initiative aims to provide a career structure for classroom practitioners and to reward performance in the classroom. This is measured against a Standard for Chartered Teacher (SCT), which defines the level of accomplishment teachers might seek to achieve after completing the Standard for Full Registration and after establishing themselves in the profession (GTCS, 2003: 5).

The purpose of the new grade of Chartered Teacher is to 'provide the best, experienced teachers with opportunities to remain in teaching, to embrace new challenges, improve their skills and practice and to be rewarded accordingly' (GTCS, 2003: 5). As Menter et al. (2004) argue, the CT initiative is very much premised on a developmental model, with CT status achieved by qualification, a specialist Master's degree through which an individual would demonstrate the achievement of the Standard for Chartered Teacher. In the SCT professional action is a central focus, underpinned by a number of interacting components: professional values and personal commitments, professional knowledge and understanding and professional and personal attributes (SEED, 2003).

Since Chartered Teacher was to be qualification based, it was clear that higher education institutions would have a central role. However it was also appropriate that both prior formal and prior experiential learning should be recognized. Consequently, two routes to achieving Chartered Teacher were developed: a programme route, delivered by an accredited provider, and an accelerated route provided by the GTCS. In the original guidelines the latter route was to be available for a limited period of time (five years) after which only the programme route would be available.

All applicants for CT must complete an entry-level self-evaluation module, which enables a teacher to reflect on their practice and plan for future progression to CT. On successful completion of this, teachers can opt for one of two routes. An experienced practitioner who has undertaken formal and experiential learning can apply directly to GTCS for CT status. This is awarded on the satisfactory submission of a reflective commentary and portfolio of evidence demonstrating how the applicant meets the Standard for Chartered Teacher. If a teacher is successful on this accelerated, accredited route, they can become a CT within a year of application and receive an incremental rise in salary of approximately £6,000. Since its introduction in 2003, 140 teachers have been awarded CT status through this route.

As we have shown with regard to threshold, the opportunities for this retrospective approach to enhance practice is limited. The affirmative processes associated with the self-evaluation against a set of standards and benchmarks can be motivating and incentivizing but there is less potential to develop and enhance practice in a focused and supported way. This crucial link between development and practice, which we argue is inherent in processes of reflection, development and enquiry, are explored more fully in the next chapter

The alternative route offered by CT providers, who are in the main HEIs, consists of a 12-module postgraduate programme of study leading to the award of a Master's degree (applicants will have already completed the entry-level module). While teachers must finance their study themselves, they receive one salary increment for every two modules successfully completed. By 2005 there were approximately 2,800 teachers studying for CT on the programme route, and 140 teachers with Chartered Teacher status.[1]

As CT programmes of study are essentially developmental, the emphasis is on change-focused action. There are three main phases to the programme: the core programme, made up of four core modules which all CT course members complete;[2] the options programme, in which teachers select four modules from a suite of modules offered on a range of pathways; and the final phase of the programme, the work-based project in which teachers can complete two smaller projects, equivalent to two modules, or one large project, equivalent to four modules. If a teacher opts to follow the programme route through part-time study, they can complete the programme within six years. However, to facilitate teachers with prior learning, it is possible to make a claim for accreditation of prior learning for up to 50 per cent of the programme (six modules). Consequently, it is possible for teachers opting for this route to achieve CT within three years.

The CT emphasis on 'change-focused action' means that all modules within the programme of study are designed to enable teachers to meet aspects of the SCT. Modules are assessed through a small-scale action research project in which a teacher takes forward an aspect of learning from the module, plans and implements a classroom-based initiative, evaluates the conduct and impact of this, and explores ways in which this can be developed further. Initial research shows that it is through such action research projects that real change is happening both to individuals and how they conceive of themselves as teachers, and to classroom practice generally. Whether such changes can be seen as leading to a new or reconstructed identity is considered fully in the following chapter.

The extent to which the accelerated, accredited route can provide teachers with opportunities for 'change-focused action' is less apparent. Certainly there is an assumption and, indeed, an expectation that teachers applying for the accelerated route are already working at this level. But, as we have discussed with regard to performance threshold, the impact of evaluating and

assessing oneself against a set of standards and competences is more affirmative. Like performance threshold, the CT accredited route does not specify a
future role for the CT. While the SCT articulates what the characteristics of a
CT should be, it is less clear about what a CT should do. Indeed, many of the
arguments from teachers opposing a performance threshold are similar to
those about CT, in particular the view held by some that Chartered Teacher
status is an entitlement that should be automatic.

If we use the frame of our three-point CPD scale to evaluate CT, we can
see that CT provides teachers with opportunities to meet two of the three
areas: reviewing practice and acquiring new skills and knowledge. However,
the third, sharing practice and experience with colleagues and new entrants
to the profession, is a fundamental weakness in the initiative.

Teachers pursuing CT status through either the accredited or programme
routes have no obligation to inform their line manager or head teacher.
Teachers' employers, the local authorities, only become aware of who is
working towards or has achieved CT when notification of salary increments
is received. There have been two consequences of this. First, in its initial
phase, for many teachers, CT was a clandestine activity, one that some teachers did not disclose even to their colleagues. Secondly, within schools, there
are no structures or frameworks required or in place to support teachers who
are working towards CT, or those who have attained it. A further tension is
that while the SCT expects collegiate activity, there are no formal mechanisms providing for this in schools (Reeves and l'Anson, 2005). As we have
argued in Chapters 6 and 7, the recasting of schools as learning communities
offers greater potential for school improvement and the enhancement of
learning and teaching, but the decoupling of CT from the school context has
limited its potential for impact, at least in its initial phase.

Chartered London Teacher

Chartered London Teacher (CLT) was launched in September 2004 and the
first such teachers will receive the status in September 2006. This status is
unique to London, and accessible only to teachers in the capital. Its purpose
is similar to the Scottish CT and AST in England and Wales, and this is 'to
recognize and reward the skills and expertise of London teachers'
(Teachernet, 2005b). Teachers pursuing CLT must demonstrate and provide
evidence that they meet the CLT standards across four main strands (Table
8.4) relating to practice, enquiry and professional development (see the CLT
website, 2005 at www.clt.ac.uk).

Table 8.4 ■ Chartered London Teacher strands

Pedagogy and pupil learning
Subject specialism and phase learning
Whole-school issues
Diversity, communities and cultures

The incentives for teachers to purse CLT status are a one-off pay reward of £1,000 and, it is claimed, the prestige of having gained outstanding status as a teacher (Teachernet, 2005b). This varies somewhat from the financial incentive associated with CT and AST and suggests that CLT may be part of a strategy associated with the teacher supply problem in the capital city and where retention of teachers is a pressing matter.

■ Conclusion

We have explored the policy imperatives leading to the reform of professional development for teachers. These have resulted in a more extended concept of CPD and its role in bringing about change and improvement. The development of new career paths, linked to CPD opportunities, is a key feature of this reform. Performance threshold, AST, ET and CT all provide opportunities for teachers to extend their professionalism and to be remunerated for this. In the past ten years, the CPD landscape has changed substantially, forcing a change in culture with regard to CPD. Teachers now have to find their place in this landscape, adapting to and responding to the changes introduced. In a climate where what it means to be a teacher is qualitatively different, it is hard for teachers to avoid reflecting on and questioning their role. How this impacts on their professional development and professional identity is explored in the next chapter.

Notes

1 Information supplied by General Teaching Council for Scotland, October 2005.
2 The core modules are the Self-evaluation Entry Module, and three others organized around the themes of learning and teaching, inclusive education and team/collegiate working.

9 | CPD: changing professional identities

Chapter outline

This chapter extends the critique of professional development and new career pathways for teachers, by exploring the contribution CPD can make to enhancing professionalism and redefining identity. By framing this in the context of the policy imperatives behind recent initiatives in CPD for teachers, the chapter also considers the extent to which these new pathways enable teachers to shape and reshape their own identity, or the extent to which they impose a carefully constructed identity on teachers.

Keywords

- School improvement agenda

- CPD framework and continuum

- Reflection

- Enquiry

■ Introduction

In Chapter 8 we considered the new models and pathways of professional development for teachers that have evolved in recent years. We suggested that this is part of a fundamental shift in what it means to be a teacher, with far-reaching implications for how teachers perceive themselves and their role, and how they are seen by others. There is broad agreement that the more coherent CPD frameworks that have evolved in the education systems within the UK in recent years, mark a qualitative difference and, arguably, improvement on other forms of teacher professional development such as INSET. The focus in this chapter is how engagement with CPD can bring about not only a change of practice, but also a change of identity.

One of the legacies of the late twentieth century is that we continue to be defined by what we do, rather than who we are. This inheritance could be said to stem from neo-conservative influences in the 1980s and first part of the 1990s, with public and private roles and persona clearly delineated. The individual's public role was to serve society, increasingly as a contributor to the burgeoning knowledge economy, while self-regulation prevailed in the private space. This is uncontested for many occupations, but for the teaching profession it is more difficult to reconcile. The emphasis in education in this period was one of targets, benchmarks and renegotiated contracts – all important aspects of performance management – defining what a teacher should do, rather than the values and attributes underpinning who a teacher is. This was a consequence of the commodification of the public servant, resulting in the low esteem with which teachers came to regard themselves, and how they were viewed by society.

In the early years of the twenty-first century there have been moves to recover and restore this, and to reclaim a professional space and place for teachers. What is interesting about this is that it is the government that has been proactive in claiming this space, rather than teachers themselves and the teaching unions. Estelle Morris's speech to the Social Market Foundation in 2001 made clear that reform of the teaching profession was a central element of New Labour's reform of the public services (Morris, 2001: 2). The teaching profession, she said, must 'renew itself and restate its claim to pre-eminence'. Her vision was for a 'fruitful and new era of trust between Government and the teaching profession' (Morris, 2001: 19).

One of the ways that this could be achieved is through engagement with professional development. There is more than a moral imperative for doing this. In the twenty-first century, the role and task of being a teacher is very different from what it was, even 30 years ago. Kevin Harris outlines the historical context for this, in somewhat grim terms:

> The present history of teachers in much of the Western world has become one of decreased status and control with relation to educational issues, loss of autonomy, worsening of conditions, loss of purpose and direction, destruction of health, increased anxiety and depression, lowering of morale, and despite a continued proliferation of policy rhetoric to the contrary, subjugation to increasing government and other external controls of schools and curricula. (Harris, 1994, in Hall, 2004: 1)

For Hall, the reality is that in school, as in other workplaces, 'teachers' work has been redesigned', and 'the skills teachers need today are different from the skills needed in the past' (Hall, 2004: 3). This very different work and world reality for teachers, tests and challenges their professional identity.

The emergence of new frameworks and structures for professional development also challenges teachers' professional identity. Teachers must now self identify against a range of new titles: Advanced Skills Teacher, Excellent Teacher, Chartered Teacher. These are often billed in the media as 'super teachers', descriptions which can cause ASTs or CTs a degree of discomfort, both in the expectations they generate and how these teachers are viewed, particularly by their colleagues. An underlying assumption is that CPD frameworks and developmental opportunities are welcomed and will be embraced by all teachers. However, career advancement, in teaching as in any profession, is potentially divisive. A further aspect to this is the pressure a teacher might feel to undertake CPD. This may reflect a changing culture, where more teachers engage with CPD opportunities, and those who choose not to, for a variety of reasons, are left behind, and, at its worst, contributes to a teaching underclass.

Research on these new forms of teacher professional development is at an early stage and tends to focus on the impact for those who have successfully navigated their way to enhanced status. The impact on those who do not succeed or who withdraw is a less explored area. Certainly there are some teachers who rather than formally withdraw, simply drift away. While it could be argued that these are the very teachers for whom engagement with structured CPD opportunities could be of most benefit, another view might be that these teachers were being forced (consciously or unconsciously) into a pathway for development that was not appropriate for them.

Another assumption is that engagement with new CPD opportunities is for the most part positive and will result in change for the good. This is not necessarily the case. In their research with primary teachers involved with the threshold process, Menter et al. (2004) concluded that it added to the sense of alienation and a loss of control for some teachers, a process started by the Education Reform Act 1988. The researchers concluded that this seemed to have 'pressed the right buttons' in terms of the professional cultures and identity of teachers (Mahony et al., 2004: 3, 5) leading them to caution about the destructive nature of threshold and the imposition of standards as a means of defining teachers (Mahony, 2004: 3, 5).

Another consequence of changes in professional development opportunities for teachers, is that teaching has ceased to be homogeneous, with a clear demarcation between those teachers who opted for school management and those who chose to remain in the classroom. Now, the latter group has become differentiated with new roles, grades, titles and status. The inherent danger in this is that the CPD continuum replaces one hierarchical system with another. This is especially the case in instances (particularly in Scotland), where management structures have been flattened and posts abolished through job sizing so that opportunities for career advancement, in the traditional sense of moving up a career ladder, are now more restricted.

Gender and age can be determinants of career development and progression. Menter et al. note this with regard to the Scottish Qualification for Headship, finding in their evaluation of it that 'there are equal opportunities issues to be considered about the ability of those with major commitments outside school to be able to undertake the programme' (2005: 19). It is certainly a salient point for programmes and initiatives such as AST and CT, which are available to a greater number of teachers. These initiatives are targeted at experienced teachers at the top of the main salary scale, who often have substantial personal commitments in addition to professional ones. These individuals are often juggling multiple roles and, arguably, several identities.

These changing forms of CPD go far beyond affirmation of what many teachers already know and their colleagues acknowledge, that they are indeed accomplished teachers. In this regard, these teachers become more than what they were previously. Central to this is the new role they play in disseminating their experience, expertise and good practice as mentors, supporters, teacher-developers, substitute or associate advisers. These new roles create and offer new and different identities for teachers.

'Accomplished' or 'expert' teachers are now terms associated with the new grades of AST and CT that have been introduced in recent years. These terms imply that teachers who attain the status of AST and CT are more than experienced teachers, and can demonstrate their accomplished practice and expertise. This may have been developed in a variety of ways but the dual processes of reflection and enquiry are central to this (see McMahon and Forde, 2005).

In seeking to understand the impact of CPD and its role in the formation and re-formation of identity, the work of Reeves and Forde with regard to the Scottish Qualification for Headship is helpful. They begin initially by locating participants in activity sets, which enables them to explore the tensions, challenges and opportunities experienced by participants. The key intersection is that of CPD, which, they note, is premised on the assumption that the practice and performance of teachers will be improved by their participation in professional development, and the school set. They suggest that the construction of practice in the SQH arises at the point of intersection of competing activity sets, leading them to assume that unless a CPD intervention is simply remedial in intent, it must represent some redefinition of professional action (Reeves and Forde, 2004: 88).

Their conclusion is that 'any change in practice on the part of one or more individuals in an activity set, is fundamentally a political issue, involving contestation over the nature of practice, hence associated issues of practitioner identity' (Reeves and Forde, 2004: 89). In other words, not only is the practitioner changed by the experience, but those around her/him are changed also. There is some evidence to support this. A teacher on the Chartered Teacher Programme in Scotland remarked on the impact of the programme both for himself and his colleagues, 'It is possible to say the programme has started to impinge on my classroom practice. There has also been an upturn in the level and amount of discussion about matters pedagogical amongst my colleagues, not necessarily directly involving me, but clearly deriving from the existence of the programme' (McMahon and Forde, 2005: 4). The existence of new forms and pathways for teachers' professional development, such as AST and CT, and the involvement of at least one teacher from most schools does appear to be leading to a change in culture with regard to CPD.

Reeves and Forde's claims are substantiated by the evaluative study of the SQH conducted by Menter et al. (2005). Research for the study showed that the programme was successful, in changing both participants and their schools, the authors concluded that the programme had been 'effective in many instances in engaging with the dynamic emotional and professional dimensions of teacher development and in contributing to school improvement' (Menter et al., 2005: 7). The research found that participants were changed by the experience. Equally important was the extent to which participants' engagement with the programme impacted on their school. In one primary school, where the acting head teacher was undertaking the SQH, it was felt that 'the professional culture of the school developed alongside her leadership skills' (Menter et al., 2005: 14). In another 'island' school, the participation of a senior teacher on the SQH programme had an extended impact, putting 'the whole school in touch with a wider professional network and brought numerous new ideas into the school' (Menter et al., 2005: 17).

Menter et al. found strong evidence of SQH candidates having their 'world view' significantly awakened by the programme and many of those interviewed for the research spoke about 'a reawakening of an interest in, and often a passion for, educational issues and debates'. They also found 'a sense of excitement and enthusiasm among candidates for ideas and for the value of reading, research and theory in education' (Menter et al., 2005: 13, 18).

The two key elements around which the SQH programme was constructed are

1 A model of practice that enabled the development of a professional and reflective approach to educational leadership and management;
2 Providing a pattern of experiences that would ensure that candidates were able to apply new learning to their work in school (Reeves et al., 2001: 203).

These two elements also underpin the Chartered Teacher programme, though the focus is on changing classroom practice rather than educational leadership and management.

Early evidence suggests that the CT programme is having a transformative effect for participants. In our research (discussed in Chapter 3), experienced classroom practitioners were asked if they felt they had distinctive professional identity and how was this shaped. One respondent felt that she/he did not have a distinctive professional identity, but that she/he was beginning to acquire this through the CT programme. This was also the view of another respondent who felt that 'Although both initial teacher education and CPD have been important, the influence, professionalism and experience of colleagues have also shaped my identity. In addition, embarking on the CT programme has been important'. The insights offered by another respondent into how professional identity has been shaped are of value in considering teachers' professional development. For this teacher, professional identity was 'shaped by ITE to a considerable extent, enhanced by CPD to some extent and developed by experience to some extent'.

The role of others – colleagues, peers and senior managers is also an important factor in shaping professional identity. One respondent felt that professional identity is inhibited 'by lack of contact with like-minded teachers who share similar values'. This teacher says that she/he would greatly appreciate the opportunity to talk with other professionals but that this opportunity does not exist for her/him. She/he suggests that 'a professional identity would surely require a body of individuals who share a common goal – unfortunately just because you work in a school it does not necessarily follow that all value the concepts of professionalism or professional identity'.

This aspect of collegiality and collaboration appears to be an important factor in bringing about a change in teachers' professional identity. Teachers opting to engage with a CPD opportunity, linked to a new career path such as AST or CT, set themselves apart from their peers. They become something other than what they were previously, in the first instance an aspiring AST or CT and then formally recognized as such. Teachers on award-bearing courses such as CT also become learners and students, with all the opportunities, challenges and demands that this brings.

Relationships with colleagues and peers can become tense, and where a work-based project requires collaboration, some teachers find their colleagues are unwilling to co-operate. This was also found to be the experience of some SQH candidates trying to elicit support from their colleagues and being told 'It's your SQH' (Reeves and Forde, 2004: 92). This potential for conflict becomes even greater on programmes such as CT, where there is clear financial gain attached. In their research on ASTs, Taylor and Jennings reported that long standing ASTs had spoken about how they had been first referred to as 'super teachers', and that this had sometimes caused resentment among colleagues (Taylor and Jennings, 2004: 11).

Recognition of status, through a new title, is an important feature of the new CPD initiatives and one that appeals to teachers. The ASTs surveyed in Taylor and Jennings's research reported that 'they felt valued and were pleased that their expertise had been recognized' (Taylor and Jennings, 2004: 11). Recognition from senior managers was an important factor for some in our research. One respondent felt that senior managers see no value in the CT concept, while another felt that her/his professional identity was inhibited by lack of recognition from the SMT about the amount of effort invested in CT courses. This is also important for ASTs and, as Taylor and Jenning's survey of 1,000 ASTs revealed, many ASTs felt that too few people knew about their work (Taylor and Jennings, 2004: 4). Thus professional validity is closely linked to public recognition.

A teacher engaging with professional development linked to a career pathway, which will result in either a new position or title, must necessarily find ways to manage and adapt to these altered and sometimes contentious professional relationships. Reeves and Forde explore the dynamics associated with this process (Reeves and Forde, 2004). With regard to the SQH, they argue that a participant operates in three social spaces, with three associated identities (Table 9.1) and these are critical to changing practice. These are:

Table 9.1

Space	Identity
The first space	Work identity
The second space	Learner identity
The third space	Changing identity

Reeves and Forde conclude that '[s]ecuring a space for change seems critical to the success of achieving the espoused outcome of CPD, i.e., changes in practice' (2004: 93).

Where a teacher finds 'a space for change' is also important. For ASTs, networks co-ordinated by local authorities were generally found to be helpful (Taylor and Jennings, 2004: 13). Network meetings provide opportunities for sharing good practice and, in some networks, ASTs make regular presentations on aspects of their work. Chartered Teacher also appears to offer classroom practitioners 'a space for change'. One course member reported 'The programme provides a forum and a focus for genuine discussion and interest in what goes on in school and in classrooms. I think the extent to which the programme does this is unprecedented and entirely welcome'. This teacher goes on to say, 'Being part of a kind of constant discourse between theory and practice is also extremely professionally reassuring, as well as interesting' (McMahon and Forde, 2005: 4). It seems then, CT offers not only a 'space for change' but 'a *safe* space for change'. As we have noted earlier, a decision to engage with further professional development initiates a process of internal and external change. This is a complex process which can cause a participant to feel professionally insecure and vulnerable, albeit temporarily.

For many CT course members, the programmes offer them a place to try out new ideas, to challenge and have challenged existing beliefs, and to examine and develop their own practice in a structured but supported way. Revisiting and engaging with educational theory and research is an important part of this, and for many teachers this is important in validifying their right to change. For Reeves this offers teachers a 'personal war machine' or critical armour (Reeves & l'Anson, 2005: 7). Thus with Forde, she argues, 'Theory and expertise become political instruments in fighting for the social space to practice differently rather than simply a matter of individual capability and know how' (Reeves and Forde, 2004: 101).

A further aspect of how engaging with professional development opportunities leading to a new career pathway can alter professional identity is the degree of personal and professional risk involved. In March 2005, GTCS conducted a survey of 6,500 teachers who had expressed an interest in CT. The survey found some expression of fear and vulnerability from respondents who hesitated in embarking on the CT programme for fear of failure and how this would impact on their professional self-esteem and standing (GTCS, 2005: 7).

Earlier, we asked at what point can we trust our professional identity and the values and beliefs it rests upon? It seems from teachers' engagement with development opportunities, validation and recognition are central in securing the new identity, which a teacher's altered status will bring. Validity, we suggest, is attained by extending one's own professional knowledge and expertise by engaging with development opportunities beyond contractual obligations. This can be the reflective analysis and evidencing of enhanced practice against a set of standards (performance threshold, AST, accredited route for CT), or the development of practice through further study and application in the classroom (award-bearing programmes, such as the CT programme route).

Recognition comes with the designation of a new title, which by its very nature is a sign that a classroom practitioner has become something else – different and greater. As we have seen, how teachers perceive themselves and others is an important element in the re-formation of professional identity. For ASTs, the key requirement is for 'excellent teaching practice and credibility with a wide range of colleagues inside and outside the school' (DfES, 2001a: 5). Consequently, interviews with managers, colleagues, parents and pupils are a feature of the assessment process to become an AST (DfES, 2001a: 13). This is a similar feature of the SQH programme in Scotland, where course members undertake a '360 degree' self-evaluation exercise, which requires input from their colleagues, as well as field visits to assess the conduct and impact of development projects.

Teachers' perception of self is shaped by engagement with professional development opportunities and the change in one's self, identity and practice may initially be harder for a teacher to see and discern. Advice from a primary head teacher to a question posted on a *TES* Online Forum from a teacher wanting to become an Advanced Skills Teacher explains this well: 'I see the Advanced Skills Teacher providing inspiration for others by being constantly adaptable, flexible and looking at the world through fresh ideas, understanding there's always another way, another approach, better resources which provide increased learning opportunities for pupils. In this respect, it's an attitude of mind' (*TES* Online Forum, 2003). Evidence from the CT programme underlines this, and CT course members often have to be encouraged to 'think like a CT'.

Clearly then, change is an inherent element of any CPD programme or initiative. For ASTs, a further dimension to this, is their role in helping other teachers change their practice. An OFSTED survey in 2003 found that ASTs spend a high proportion of their time advising other teachers on class organization and teaching methods, and helping those who are experiencing difficulties in their teachers (OFSTED, 2003: 8). OFSTED noted that there was a considerable change in emphasis in their role from the time of the previous inspection, 2001 (OFSTED, 2003: 5), with both secondary and primary ASTs participating significantly in initial teacher training and in work with newly qualified teachers.

In both surveys in 2001 and 2003, OFSTED inspectors raised concerns about provision for the training and development needs of ASTs. In the 2003 survey it was found that only around half of the ASTS had received specific training for their role. In 2001, OFSTED noted that

> ASTs have a number of training and communication needs. They often
> need further guidance on what is, and what is not appropriate AST work
> and how to go about carrying it out. Consideration needs to be given to
> establishing a national network which might go a long way to alleviating
> the isolation felt by many ASTs. (OFSTED, 2001: 11)

These concerns remained in the 2003 survey, and the inspectors noted that 'arrangements for the performance management and professional development of ASTs pay far too little attention to the distinctive features of their role' (OFSTED, 2003: 15).

For ASTs then it could be said that the focus is one of developing others, rather than, or before, developing self. If this is the case, and the evidence from OFSTED and Taylor and Jennings's research suggests it is, the change to professional identity is more complex for ASTs. Indeed, it is the role of teacher-developer that seems to generate most insecurity for ASTs. Taylor and Jennings's research found that most ASTs regard their role as teacher-developer, in terms of encouragement and inspiration. They found a marked reluctance to identify weaknesses in the performance of other teachers and challenge them to improve their practice. Advanced Skills Teachers participants in the research expressed a reluctance to observe teachers for the purpose of assessment or identifying training needs (Taylor and Jennings, 2004: 11).

It could be argued that through the teacher-developer aspect of their post, ASTs are being forced into a role that they find difficult to identify with, and for which they are not fully prepared. Assisting others to develop and enhance their practice may also bring personal benefit to an AST, and indeed this is often the case, but the nature of the task and time frame for achieving it tends not to offer the AST with a 'safe space for change' both for the teacher they are assisting and for themselves. While there may be opportunities and occasions for reflection, the level of critical reflection and engagement the task may require is often not available to the AST.

Teachers recognize the limitations of superficial engagement with reflection. One teacher, responding to a question on opportunities for reflection for our research, believed that reflection is 'utterly essential'. They also recognize that reflection is a learned skill and report that, 'Much of the reflection I observe during in-service days is not deeply reflective, with conclusions backed by evidence. Indeed it tends to be superficial and unsubstantiated'. Another teacher's response was 'We do not really get much time for reflection – it would be useful if we did. Occasional INSET days are really too contrived to be effective'. For one teacher who had engaged with critical reflection as part of the CT programme, they found that it 'Facilitated more effective learning and teaching; facilitated enhanced ability to deal with behavioural difficulties; improved ability to relate to colleagues, provide support and resolve issues'.

■ Conclusion

Teaching is a changed and changing profession. This is evident throughout the education sector, in curriculum reform, in how teachers are prepared for their future role by initial teacher education and in the opportunities available for professional development. Engagement with CPD can and does bring about change, at an individual, collective and institutional level. However the extent of that change, and consequently the impact of it, is very much related to the form of professional development. We have suggested that essential elements for this are *reflection and enquiry*. Current forms of professional development, linked to career advancement, provide both of these to a greater or less extent. Affirmative processes, such as threshold or the CT accreditation route are limited in their ability to bring about long-term change, unless there are further structures and opportunities to facilitate this. Advanced Skills Teacher and ET offer a new professional status and role, but the extent to which this comes about through reflection and enquiry is limited. While AST might offer a greater potential for impact, through the outreach aspect of the role, what is possible is constrained by the nature of the role and preparation for it. Chartered Teacher, constructed on a model of reflective practice, offers the greater opportunity for change through reflection and enquiry, but the lack of a defined role for the Chartered Teacher reduces the potential for impact in the wider context of the school organization.

In some respects, the forms of professional development and career advancement currently available to teachers fall short of an ideal model of professional development centred on reflection and enquiry. The opportunities for professional development outlined only partially meet the three-point scale we used to discuss CPD in the previous chapter (reviewing practice, acquiring new skills and knowledge, and sharing good practice and experience with colleagues and new entrants to the profession). As we have shown in Chapters 6 and 7, professional development for teachers cannot be disassociated from the classroom and school context since these are the precise locus for the work of teachers. What is required is an integrated and holistic approach to CPD that enables the practitioner to reflect on and develop his/her practice in a way that is relevant to the situational context but which supports the practitioner as she/he engages in the professional and personal processes of change that are associated with this.

CONCLUSION

10   Professional development, reflection and enquiry

Chapter outline

In this chapter we argue that professional development, reflection and enquiry are the means by which teachers can fulfil their role in a highly complex and constantly changing world, in a way that is meaningful, productive and rewarding for teachers and their pupils. The model we propose is one of the engaged professional, or the engaged teacher. This model challenges and extends existing models. In this chapter, we make a case for a reconsideration of how we prepare and support teachers for their critical role in educating young people today.

Keywords

- Education policy

- Policy community

- Policy futures

■ Introduction

Currently, the demographic profile of the profession indicates that significant numbers of teaching staff across education sectors are retiring or leaving the profession. This situation affects teachers, school leaders, teacher educators, educational administrators and our education systems in general because of the consequent loss of experience and expertise. This is only one of the challenges that the teaching profession faces. We have argued that one way to retain staff may be to enable them to build a more robust sense of professional identity, and to develop a professional sense of self which is part of a recognized and valued community of practice.

Other challenges lie in the policy arena. While each of the UK education systems has a distinctive set of education policies, there is substantial 'policy borrowing' (Phillips and Ochs, 2003). In each system the dominant discourse over recent years has been one of performativity. As we have seen from earlier chapters, there has been development in detail of advice, sets of guidelines and regulations shaping classroom activity within each system. While attention remains narrowly focused on attainment data as the measure of performance, there is a danger that a more rounded consideration of effectiveness in teaching and learning is lost.

Challenges also lie in the shifting of the professional agenda towards the concept of 'new professionalism'. This implies the reconstruction of teacher professionalism and identity, and we have argued that the continuing professional development of teachers is pivotal to this. More expansive explorations of teaching and learning as the basis for both initial education and continuing development of teachers is critical if the potential of ideas such as 'professional learning communities' and 'teacher leadership' is to be realized. This leaves us with some questions about future policy in education:

- How should we construct the accountability of teachers?
- How should future education policy in the UK systems be constructed?
- How should teachers be engaged in decision-making processes and what should be the nature of the relationship between different levels of decision-making?

We look at each of these areas with a view to discussing how teachers' professional development is vital to the construction not just of the teaching profession, but of education policy itself. In doing this, we accept that with agency comes accountability. How then are we to develop teacher accountability within future education policy?

■ Constructing the accountability of teachers

In Chapter 4 we discussed the legacy of the discourse of derision on teacher professionalism. We argued that the notion of a halcyon era of teacher autonomy is misplaced. We also referred to the work of Rutter et al. (1979) and their findings on school effectiveness and school improvement. Against a backdrop where some schools were and are deemed to perform less effectively than other schools in similar circumstances, a lack of external accountability is no longer tenable. Further, as Johnson and Hallgarten (2002: 5) argue:

The essential paradox is that during this period of demoralisation due to workload and loss of autonomy, teachers, particularly primary, have improved their skills and transformed their performance. Very detailed planning of every lesson, and execution with absolute concentration on the individual attainment of those central targets, has led to continuous improvement in pupil attainment in the areas tested.

A greater focus on the learning and achievement of individual pupils, a greater sense of considering the holistic development and care of the pupil, and a repositioning of the pupil as an agent in her/his own learning, are trends we mapped out in earlier chapters. These, we argued, call for change in the behaviours of teachers and ultimately in how they construct their identities.

In order to support this process we need to reconceptualize professional decision-making and the collective role of teachers in designing and developing teaching and learning at school level, local authority level and national level. We are not urging a retreat to recapture an idealized version of teacher autonomy, but rather a process in which the teaching profession is allowed to engage in the development of public policy. In this way individual teachers will feel a deeper connectedness to the policy they must implement. Johnson and Hallgarten (2002: 13) argue that the keynote of policy development and implementation should now be a question of 'subsidiarity, the principle that different kinds of decisions should be made at different levels'.

Johnson and Hallgarten's principle of subsidiarity raises some significant issues. We could look at decision-making at two main levels:

- Why any particular change process is to be implemented.
- How particular change processes are implemented within the school and the classroom.

The first question – the 'why' question – is in the educational systems in the UK determined at government level, either national or local government through policies and guidelines. That does not mean to say that staff in schools should not consider issues of purpose and philosophy. Indeed such debates are an essential feature of a professional learning community. However, equally important is the question 'how' should a policy directive be implemented and it is here that an initiative can be nuanced to take into account the particular circumstances of a school, its goals and the understandings and skills of teachers. It is in this arena that we should look to increasing the active participation of teachers exercising their professional judgement.

We are facing in the UK what the OECD (2005) has described as a once in a generation chance of refreshing the profile of the teaching profession. However, this chance comes with a challenge: do we want to enable teachers to have agency over their profession, and do we want this agency to extend into educational decision-making, at school level and at policy level?

Within an age of change and challenge, there are several choices facing the teaching profession:

■ To retreat – this involves the harking back to a time when a teacher experienced autonomy.
■ To react– a repeat of the militancy of the 1970s and 1980s with mass disaffection evident in the teaching profession and wholesale resistance to government policy.
■ To adapt – developing a professionalism-based conformity and compliance with a limited role for CPD linked to policy implementation.
■ To contribute – a strengthening of teacher participation at all levels of education and particularly at school level where ideas of participation in policy and decision-making become central.

We would argue that retreat, reaction and adaptation are all limited. Contribution at least allows teacher professionalism to become more central. But for us, there is another choice that can be advocated:

■ To create – the development of innovative practice by teachers within classrooms through professional development opportunities based on reflection and enquiry.

This last choice encourages teachers to create and lead change within schools, but to do so within a context of evidence-based practice. But engaging teachers in this role demands a reconceptualization of their place within the professional and policy community. To do this, we must decide what role teachers should play in the future of education policy and practice in the UK.

■ The future of education policy: including the teaching profession

Education must be oriented towards the future, and so must education policy. Education services have the task of providing learning experiences that are valuable and rewarding to learners, but they also have the task of preparing learners for their future, whether this is at a personal level, or whether it concerns occupational, social and democratic roles. We have to recognize that 'the teaching profession is a key mediating agency for society as it endeavours to cope with change and upheaval' (OECD, 2005: 27).

However, the Organisation for Economic Co-operation and Development (OECD, 2001: 3) suggests that 'forward-looking methodologies have been developed in only a rudimentary fashion in education compared to other sectors'. This is a salutary reminder that children who have lived only in the twenty-first century, and for whom the twentieth century is already history, have now entered the school system in the UK. A critical question facing the education system is, how should we prepare children for a tomorrow we cannot yet conceive?

Teacher policy is a concern not just across the national systems of the UK but internationally too. The OECD conducted an international study, 'Attracting, Developing and Retaining Effective Teachers', between 2002 and 2004 which found that teacher policy was high on national agendas across the 25 countries involved in the project. The OECD (2005: 12–14) also found a number of common policy directions:

- emphasizing teacher quality over teacher quantity
- developing teacher profiles to align teacher development and performance with school needs
- viewing teacher development as a continuum
- making teacher education more flexible
- transforming teaching into a knowledge rich profession
- providing schools with more responsibility for teacher personnel management.

From this, there seem to be two pivotal ideas. First, there is the centrality of teacher development and, secondly, the contextualized nature of teacher development and practice within specific schools. Importantly though, these are strategies designed not just to 'improve' the current workforce but, as we argued earlier, to retain and attract people into the profession. But how can these strategies work successfully within a robust bureaucratic and market model which stresses accountability regimes? Has the time now come for the balance to be redressed by placing teacher development at the centre of policy and retention strategies?

Over the next five to ten years there will be significant waves of retirement but '[t]he entry of significant numbers of teachers with up-to-date skills and fresh ideas has the potential to substantially renew the schools' (OECD, 2005: 18). However, indicators of support for renewal are not good.

On the one hand, some education policy has indicated the importance of teacher development. In England following the Time for Standards report, the Remodelling of the Teacher Workforce, and in Scotland the McCrone Agreement, there has been a central theme of developing a highly skilled workforce in teaching. But how far does such policy advocate and lead to a developmental approach to professional development as opposed to further training within an agenda of inflexible accountability procedures?

If we are critical of some current trends in education policy in the UK, how might future policy be conceived, and how can teachers and schools be included in a policy community? The OECD report puts forward future scenarios for schools based on three trends:

1 *The status quo extrapolated* – a continuation and intensification of current education structures where education policy is linked strongly to economic policy and, in particular, to ideas about performance and competitiveness in educational provision.
2 *Re-schooling scenarios* – the education system is repositioned within wider social policy and the public sector as the means to achieve social reconstruction and equity.
3 *De-schooling scenarios* – the education system becomes fragmented with more informal, dispersed and flexible learning opportunities available.

We can therefore explore some of the implications within each of these scenarios, and a critical question here is, *what would be the position of the teacher and the construction of professionalism* within each of these? If we are to look at the future position of the teacher within policy formation and practice we must ask how the various options might impact upon teacher professionalism and professional identity. The future is not determined: the government can choose to encourage teacher agency, teacher policy development, and to do so within a system where schools develop as learning communities. To choose not to do this would risk following scenarios that may continue to narrow the focus of what it is to be a teacher, and to limit pupils' opportunities for meaningful learning.

If we look at the OECD scenarios in more depth, we can see that each has repercussions for teacher development – not all of which are positive.

The Status Quo Extrapolated

Scenario 1: Robust bureaucratic school systems

- Strong bureaucracies and robust institutions.
- Nested interests resist fundamental change.
- Continuing problems of school image and resourcing.

Impact on teacher identity and development:

- Focus on the role of the teacher with centrally determined regulations covering the curriculum, pedagogy and assessment.
- Professional identity linked with policy delivery.

Scenario 2: Extending the market model

- Widespread dissatisfaction leads to reshaping public funding and school systems.
- Rapid growth of demand-driven 'market currencies', indicators and accreditation.
- Greater diversity of providers and professionals, greater inequality.

Impact on teacher identity and development:

- Focus on teacher performance by measurable outcomes.
- Teacher development predicated on narrow aim of improving standards.
- Teacher development tends to be seen as 'training'.

Re-schooling scenarios

Scenario 3: Schools as core social services

- High levels of public trust and funding.
- Schools as centres of community and social capital formation.
- Greater organizational/professional diversity, greater social equity.

Impact on teacher identity and development:

- Focus on the teacher working in interdisciplinary teams – blurring of the professional demarcation working in community-based facilities.

Scenario 4: Schools as focused learning organizations

- High levels of public trust and funding.
- Schools and teachers network widely in learning.
- Strong quality and equity features.

Impact on teacher identity and development:

- Focus on teachers as a profession with specialist and highly developed skills working in communities of practice.
- Teacher professional identity no longer seen as being developed in isolation.

De-schooling scenarios

Scenario 5: Learner networks and the network society

- Widespread dissatisfaction with/rejection of organized school systems.
- Non-formal learning using ICT potential to reflect the 'network society'.
- Communities of interest, potential serious equity problems.

Impact on teacher identity and development:

- Dispersal of the teaching profession across a range of learning and training organizations and groups.
- Identity becomes individualistic.

Scenario 6: Teacher exodus – the 'meltdown' scenario

- Severe teacher shortages do not respond to policy action.
- Retrenchment, conflict and falling standards leading to areas of 'meltdown'.
- Crisis may provide spur to widespread innovation but future still uncertain.

Impact on teacher identity and development:

- Increased low morale and stress, lack of status for teachers and failure to recruit into the teaching profession.
- Few incentives (personal or professional) to engage in identity formation and development.

These scenarios help us to consider a range of possibilities for the future of the teaching profession. Our preferred option is scenario 4, which seems to refocus education as a social concern and a potential social good. Is there evidence that the education policy agenda under New Labour is moving us towards this scenario?

In 2001, the Labour government's vision for the educational systems in England and Wales was set out in the report *Professionalism and Trust*. The title at least sounds more hopeful. The report recognizes the fractured relationships between government and the teaching profession but at the same time, the accountability agenda is strongly presented:

> There is no doubt that Governments over the last 30 years have not always rushed to express their confidence in teachers. But we are leaving those days behind and entering a new and positive era.

> It is important to trust our professionals to get on with the job. That does not mean leaving professionals to go their own way, without scrutiny – we shall always need the constant focus on effective teaching and learning, and the accountability measures described above. But what it does mean is that we shall increasingly want to see professionals at the core, to join us in shaping the patterns for the schools of the future. (DfES, 2001b: 27)

This thread has continued within more recent policy objectives.

Certainly education policy in the UK has shifted the nature of the relationship between government and teachers from the 1980s to the early twenty-first century. But in our view the shift has occurred firmly within scenarios 1 and 2, combining robust bureaucracy with the market model of delivery. Barber (2002) sees four stages to this changing relationship:

1 Uninformed professional judgement until the mid-1980s: teacher goodwill but no direction.
2 Uninformed prescription – the response of the Thatcherite governments to tackle underperformance.
3 Informed prescription – in the first Labour government post-1997 using the data and evidence about best practice which have become steadily more powerful, but where 'teachers perceived the changes as imposed from outside and worried about the degree to which they could tailor and adapt the government's materials to their own purposes' (Barber, 2002: n.p.).
4 A new era of informed professional judgements.

Barber, in this speech, refers to 'intelligent accountabilities', and we would to some extent agree that this is necessary, but it depends how the idea is fully conceptualized and what model of teacher development it includes. A seemingly developmental approach has also become the keynote of the latest policy document in Scotland: *Ambitious, Excellent Schools* (SEED, 2004a). Does this mean a sea change in both policy and attitude towards the teaching profession?

However, Alexander's (2004: 7) highly critical appraisal of both Barber's paper and of the policy strategy the speech was launching, argues that the strategy is still endorsing 'a culture of pragmatism and compliance' and that the teacher's professional judgement in relation to pedagogic matters is still open to policy diktat. It needs to be borne in mind that Barber's analysis came out of his role as Head of the Prime Minister's Delivery Unit. His paper (Barber, 2002) ends with this comment on the Blair government's record:

> Much has been done since 1997 … Much more will be necessary, including attending to lifestyle, career progression and professional development as well as enabling teachers to be well-rewarded while remaining classroom teachers. The extensive reforms of the teaching profession, including the introduction of performance-related pay, have laid the foundations for this, but it is only the beginning. The status of the teaching profession should be enhanced by the shape of the era of informed professional judgement.

There is then, within this brave new world of informed judgement still to be a focus on performance measurement. How else can there be performance-related pay? And how does the notion of performance-related pay link to a model of teacher professional development that asks teachers to enquire and develop in the broadest meanings of these terms?

One of the criticisms of the *Schools Driving Forward Change* report (OPSR/DfES, 2002) in England is that of micromanagement. Policies are now emphasizing more autonomy for schools and the freeing of teachers to do what they do best. However, what has still to be determined are the parameters of this flexibility. The central theme of this book has been to consider the circumstances which would enable teachers to forge new identities and so be able to reclaim their profession. Unless teachers have the space and the opportunity to do this the ideal of informed professional judgement will be difficult to realize. Government policy in England and Wales, as well as that in Scotland, has some way to go if it is to move towards an endorsement of the models of schooling and teacher professionalism seen in OECD scenarios 3 and 4. The danger of retaining a focus on bureaucracy and market principles is that the profession becomes oriented to delivery and performance, rather than being seen as a key element in framing policy and helping to decide on the future of schools.

■ Engaging teachers in decision-making

In a democratic society, a public service such as education, funded through the public purse should be open to scrutiny and to some direction by the government. However, at another level we can point to instances of resistance by the teaching profession to specific changes where it was judged that these were more about political doctrine than about the learning experiences of pupils. The debates and campaigns surrounding the introduction of national testing in Scotland in the early 1990s are a noteworthy example, where teacher unions and associations allied with parent groups in a campaign to resist the proposals to bring in national testing (Simpson, 2005). This campaign resulted in a modified programme in which teacher judgement played a significant role in determining the readiness and timing of the use of national tests.

Even in less controversial areas, the position of teachers in taking proposals forward is vital. It would be inaccurate to paint a picture of policy-making within education over the past 20 years as a process in which the teacher's voice has been entirely excluded. The vast array of policies and guidelines is produced by working groups that routinely involve practitioners. However, the presence of one or two teachers on a committee – at local or national level – does not create deeper *connectedness* for individual teachers working in schools. Most teachers who have to implement policy will not have been part of the policy or curriculum creation, or will have had only marginal involvement. For them, the policy becomes another document or another teaching pack downloaded to the classroom for them to implement. Any questioning of the process is often construed as teachers resisting change.

However, a core element of professionalism is surely the ability to make choices in relation to the needs of the client. *The Statement of Professional Values and Practice for Teachers* (GTCE, 2004b: 2) notes: 'Teachers have insight into the learning needs of young people. They use professional judgement to meet those needs and to choose the best ways of motivating pupils to achieve success. They use assessment to inform and guide their work.' Further, there seems to be an obligation for any professional to consider the needs of the client, and to consider how policy and practice affects them. Such consideration should be at an individual and collective level. But to do this would involve opening up key policy and practice to debate, discussion and contestation. There are undoubted risks involved for the policy-makers as well as for individual teachers and school leaders in doing this. Tensions of the sort we explored in Chapter 6 may result.

Nevertheless debate and discussion should become the core processes of *reflection and enquiry* within a professional learning community. Without this type of debate any implementation process will be largely superficial and exclude rather than include professional groups. Instead of being constructed as teachers unwillingly embracing new ideas, we should reconceptualize debate as 'sense-making' and recognize its importance in the development of teaching and learning. Sense-making is a process by which we understand a new situation and construct meaning. The more flexible the processes of reflection and enquiry collectively or individually, the more likely there will be sense-making to deal with the unexpected: 'making something sensible'.

Here the idea is not about interpreting policy or programmes as constructed by groups or bodies external to the organization and then solving the problem of how to implement them in a particular situation, but is more about 'problem-setting'. It is essentially a proactive process. As Weick (1995: 11) argues: '[a] crucial property of sensemaking is that human situations are progressively clarified, but this clarification often works in reverse. It is less often the case that an outcome fulfills some prior definition of the situation, and more often the case that an outcome *develops* that prior definition'. Ultimately then, this is a creative process in which proposed changes are constructed and shaped within a particular context to look to the process of how proposals are taken forward.

Deciding how proposals should progress is something that can be dealt with at different levels – both as a whole school and with individual teachers. Collective decision-making is first about consistency, but secondly it promotes ideas of community and of community ownership of professional policy and practice. Ownership is something that has been underestimated in education policy, which often tends to rely on the production of a specific type of knowledge by teachers, a knowledge that centres on implementation rather than creation and adaptation. Policy initiatives are often accompanied by additional guidelines for practice in which there are examples of 'good practice'. Although the production of these materials is well intentioned, they may seem over-idealized or distant from the realities of a particular school and the day-to-day lives of teachers in classrooms. There is work to be done to make these ideas practical in the particular context of a school and then into a specific classroom environment. Once again, this is the core of the process of 'teacher leadership'.

For us, models of teacher involvement must centre on the school and the classroom, and these locations should be the focal point of professional development, reflection and enquiry. If it is to be meaningful, policy creation as well as implementation has to have teacher professionalism at its heart. However, we must move into a new era of teacher professionalism, where teachers are enabled and trusted to work within their schools to create communities of practice, certainly within frameworks of accountability, but of accountability that is more focused on teaching and learning than on simplistic measures of performance. To return to Day et al. (2005: 576), the challenge for policy-makers is 'to create contexts in which teachers can make connections between the priorities of the school and their individual, personal, professional and collective identity'. It is time for education policy to move in a different direction: not just to include the profession in its creation, but to drive forward a model of teacher professionalism that could ultimately lead to more fulfilling educational experiences for pupils and for teachers in our schools.

Bibliography

Admiraal, W. and Wubbels, T. (2005) Multiple voices, multiple realities, what truth? Student teachers learning to reflect in different paradigms, *Teachers and Teaching: Theory and Practice*, 11(3): 315–29.

Ainscow, M., Booth, T. and Dyson, A. (2003) *Understanding and Developing Inclusive Practices in School*, Final Report ESRC, TLRP Phase 1 Network, www.esrcsocietytoday.ac.uk/ ESRCInfoCentre/ViewAwardPage.aspx?AwardId=1011, accessed 26 October 2005.

Alcorn, M. (2005) 'Eight stages of Excellence' *Times Educational Supplement Scotland*, www.tes.co.uk/search/story/?story_id=2097304 (accessed 16/01/06).

Alexander, R. (2004) Still no pedagogy? Principle, pragmatism and compliance in primary education, *Cambridge Journal of Education*, 34(1): 7–33.

Andersson, E.P. (1993) The perspective of student nurses and their perceptions of professional nursing during the nurse training programme, *Journal of Advanced Nursing*, 18: 808–15.

Apple, M.W. and Beane, J.A. (1999) The case for democratic schools, in M.W. Apple and J.A. Beane (eds), *Democratic Schools: Lessons from the Chalk Face*. Buckingham: Open University Press. pp. 1–29.

Atkinson, D. (2004) Theorising how student teachers form their identities in initial teacher education, *British Educational Research Journal*, 30(3): 379–94.

Avis, J. (1994) Teacher professionalism: one more time … *Educational Review*, 46(1): 63–72.

Avis, J. (2003) Re-thinking trust in a performative culture: the case of education, *Journal of Education Policy*, 18(3): 315–32.

Avis, J. (2005) Beyond performativity: reflections on activist professionalism and the labour process in further education. *Journal of Education Policy*, 20(2): 209–22.

Ball, S. (1990) *Politics and Policy Making in Education: Explorations in Policy Sociology*. London: Routledge

Ball, S. (2003) The teacher's soul and the terrors of performativity, *Journal of Education Policy*, 18(2): 215–28.

Bandura, A. (2000) Exercise of human agency through collective efficacy, *Current Directions in Psychological Science*, 9(3): 75–8.

Barber, M. (2002) The next stage for large scale reform in England: from good to great, paper presented at the Technology Colleges Trust Vision 2020 Second International Conference, www.cybertext.net.au/tct2002/disc_papers/organisation/barber.htm, accessed 5 October 2005.

Barratt, E. (2004), Foucault and the politics of critical management studies, *Culture and Organisation*, 10(3): 191–202.

Barth, R. (2001) *Learning by Heart*, San Francisco, CA: Jossey-Bass.

Bartlett, S. (2002) An evaluation of the work of group of best practice teacher researchers, *Journal of In-Service Education*, 28(3): 527–41.

Bartlett, L. (2004) Expanding teacher work roles: a resource for retention or a recipe for overwork? *Journal of Education Policy*, 19(5): 565–82.

Begley, C.M. and White, P. (2003) Irish nursing students' changing self-esteem and fear of negative evaluation during their preregistration programme, *Journal of Advanced Nursing*, 42(4): 390–401.

Beijaard, D., Verloop, N. and Vermunt, J. (2000) Teachers' perceptions of professional identity: an exploratory study from a personal knowledge perspective, *Teaching and Teacher Education*, 16(2): 750.

Besley, A.C. (2005a) Jim Marshall: Foucault and disciplining the self, *Educational Philosophy and Theory*, 37(3): 309–15.

Besley, A.C. (2005b) Self-denial or self-mastery? Foucault's genealogy of the confessional self, *British Journal of Guidance & Counselling*, 33(3): 365–82.

Beynon, J., Ilieva, R. and Dichupa, M. (2001) Teachers of Chinese ancestry: interaction of identities and professional roles, *Teacher Education*, 12(2): 135–51.

Blair, T. (1999) Speech to Party Conference, Bournemouth.

Bottery, M. (2003) The leadership of learning communities in a culture of unhappiness, *School Leadership and Management*, 23(2): 187–207.

Brown, G. (2005) *Prosperity and justice for all*, Speech, Labour Party Conference, Brighton Centre, 27 September, www.labour.org.uk/index.php?id=news&ux_news_id=ac04gb, accessed 26 October 2005.

Bruner, J. (1990) *Acts of Meaning*. London: Harvard University Press.

Bryce, T.G.K. and Humes, W.M. (2003) *Scottish Education. Second Edition Post Devolution*, Edinburgh: Edinburgh University Press.

Burnard, P. (1995) Nurse educators' perceptions of reflection and reflective practice, *Journal of Advanced Nursing*, 21(6): 1167–74.

Caldwell, B.J. and Spinks, J.M. (1988) *The Self-Managing School*. London: Falmer Press.

Callaghan, J. (1976) Towards a national debate, Ruskin College Speech, http://education.guardian.co.uk/ thegreatdebate/story/0,9860,574645,00.html, accessed 18 July 2005.

Central Advisory Council for England (CACE) (1967) *Children and their Primary Schools: A Report of the Central Advisory Council for England. Vol. 1.* (Plowden Report). London: HMSO.

Chan, D.W. (2002) Stress, self-efficacy, social support, and psychological distress among prospective Chinese teachers in Hong Kong, *Educational Psychology*, 22(5): 557–69.

Chapman, D.W. and Green, M.S. (1986) Teacher retention: a further examination, *Journal of Educational Research*, 79(5): 273–9.

Clayton, T. (1993) 'From Domestic Helper to "Assistant Teacher" ': the changing role of the British classroom assistant, *European Journal of Special Needs Education*, 8(1): 32–44.

Cochran-Smith, M. (2000) The future of teacher education: framing the questions that matter, *Teaching Education*, 11(1): 13–24.

Coldron, J. and Smith, R. (1999) Active location in teachers' construction of their professional identities, *Journal of Curriculum Studies*, 31(6): 711–26.

Committee of Enquiry into the Education of Handicapped Children and Young People (CEEHCYP) (1978) *Special Educational Needs*, Report of Committee of Enquiry into the Education of Handicapped Children and Young People (Warnock Report). London: HMSO.

Committee of Inquiry into Professional Conditions of Service for Teachers (2000) *A Teaching Profession for the 21st Century (The McCrone Report) Volume 1*. Edinburgh: The Stationery Office.

Committee to Review Assessment in the Third and Fourth Years of Secondary Education in Scotland (CRATFYSES) (1977) *Assessment for All: Report of the Committee to Review Assessment in the Third and Fourth Years of Secondary Education in Scotland* (Dunning Report). Edinburgh: HMSO.

Coolahan, J. (2002) *Teacher Education and the Teaching Career in an Era of Lifelong Learning*, OECD Education Working Paper No. 2, www.olis.oecd.org/OLIS/2002DOC. NSF/LINKTO/EDU-WKP(2002)2, accessed 26 October 2005).

Cordingley, P., Bell, M., Thomason, S. and Firth, A. (2005) The impact of collaborative continuing professional development (CPD) on classroom teaching and learning. EPPI, REEL, http://eppi.ioe.ac.uk/EPPIWeb/home.aspx?page=/reel/review_groups/ CPD/review_two.htm, accessed 30 September 2005.

Cotton, A.H. (2001) Private thoughts in public spheres: issues in reflection and reflective practices in nursing, *Journal of Advanced Nursing*, 36(4): 512–19.

Cotton, P. and Hart, P.M. (2003) Occupational well-being and performance: a review of organisational health research, *Australian Psychologist*, 38(2): 118–27.

Cowan, R. (1996) Performativity, post-modernity and the university, *Comparative Education*, 32 (2): 245–58.

Crowther, F. and Olsen, P. (1997) Teachers as leaders – an exploratory framework, *International Journal of Educational Management*, 11(1): 6–13.

Davis, J. (2002) The Inner London Education Authority and the William Tyndale Junior School affair, 1974–1976, *Oxford Review of Education*, 28(2–3): 275–98.

Day, C. (2000) Effective leadership and reflective practice, *Reflective Practice*, 1(1): 113–27.

Day, C., Elliot, B. and Kington, A. (2005) Reform, standards and teacher identity: challenges of sustaining commitment, *Teaching and Teacher Education*, 21(5): 563–77.

De Lima, J.A. (2003) Trained for isolation: the impact of departmental cultures on student teachers' views and practices of collaboration, *Journal of Education for Teaching*, 29(3): 197–218.

Department for Education and Employment (DfEE) (1998) *Teachers: Meeting the Challenge of Change*. London: HMSO.

Department for Education and Employment (DfEE) (2001) *Learning and Teaching: A Strategy for Professional Development:* London: DfEE.

Department for Education and Skills (DfES) (2001a) *Advanced Skills Teachers Promoting Excellence*. London: DfES. Available at www.teachernet.gov.uk/docbank /index.cfm?id =3479 (accessed 16/01/06).

Department for Education and Skills (DfES) (2001b) *Professionalism and Trust.* London: DfES, www.teachernet.gov.uk/_doc/1042/SMF_Report.pdf, accessed 10 October 2005.

Department for Education and Skills (DfES). (2001c). *Learning and teaching: A strategy for professional development.* London: DfEE.

Department for Education and Skills (DfES) (2002) *Time for Standards: Reforming the School Workforce.* London: DfES.

Department for Education and Skills (DfES) (2003) *Raising Standards and tackling workload: a national agreement.* Available at www.teachernet.gov.uk/docbank/index.cfm?id =3479 (accessed 16/01/06).

Department for Education and Skills (DfES) (2004) *Statistics of Education: School Workforce in England.* London: HMSO.

Department for Education and Skills (DfES) (2005a) *Harnessing Technology: Transforming Learning and Children's Services.* London: DfES.

Department for Education and Skills (DfES) (2005b) *Performance Threshold.* London: DfES, www.tcachernet.gov.uk/management/payandperformance/performancethreshold/?353569083f9df74-52455889-c374-4e9b-8770-45f6cec5354f, accessed 10 October 2005.

Department for Education and Skills (DfES) (2005c) AST Guidance. London: DfES (accessed 26/10/06).

Department of Education for Northern Ireland (DENI) (2004a) *Teachers' Pay and Conditions of Service Inquiry Final Report – Part 2 Improving Conditions, Raising Standards and Negotiating Arrangements.* Belfast: DENI.

Department of Education for Northern Ireland (DENI) (2004b) *What might 'enhanced practice' look like in the future?* Briefing Paper 9, Empowering Schools in Northern Ireland, www.empoweringschools.com/briefingInfo.asp?id=14, accessed 26 October 2005.

Department of Education, Science and Training (DEST) (2000) *Teachers for the 21st Century: Making the Difference.* Australia: DEST.

DeMulder, E.K. and Rigsby, L.C. (2003) Teachers' voices on reflective practice, *Reflective Practice,* 4(3): 267–90.

Downie, R. (1990) Professions and professionalism, *Journal of Philosophy of Education,* 24(2): 147–59.

Earley, P. and Bubb, S. (2004) *Leading and Managing Continuing Professional Development.* London: Paul Chapman Publishing.

Eco-schools (n.d.) What is eco-schools? Eco-schools Programme UK, www.eco-schools.org.uk/, accessed 26 October 2005.

Evans, L. (1999) *Managing to Motivate.* London: Cassell.

Evers, W.J.G., Brouwers, A. and Tomic, W. (2002) Burnout and self-efficacy: a study on teachers' beliefs when implementing an innovative educational system in the Netherlands, *British Journal of Educational Psychology,* 72: 227–43.

Fisher, C.D. (2000) Mood and emotions while working: missing pieces of job satisfaction? *Journal of Organizational Behavior,* 21: 185–202.

Forrester, G. (2000) Professional autonomy versus managerial control: the experiences of teachers in an English primary school, *International Studies in Sociology of Education,* 10(2): 133–51.

Foucault, M. (1977) *Discipline and Punish*. London: Penguin Books.

Fraser, H., Draper, J. and Taylor, W. (1998) The quality of teachers' professional lives: teachers and job satisfaction, *Evaluation and Research in Education*, 12(2): 61–71.

Friedman, I. (2003) Self-efficacy and burnout in teaching: the importance of interpersonal relations efficacy, *Social Psychology of Education*, 6: 191–215.

Frost, D. and Harris, A. (2003) Teacher leadership: towards a research agenda, *Cambridge Journal of Education*, 33(3): 480–95.

Fullan, M. (1992) *What's Worth Fighting for in Headship*. Buckingham: Open University Press.

Furlong, J. (2005) New Labour and teacher education: the end of an era, *Oxford Review of Education*, 31(1): 119–34.

Gardner, H. (1984) *Frames of Mind: The Theory of Multiple Intelligence*. London: Fontana.

Gardner, P. (1995) Teacher training and changing professional identity in early twentieth century England, *Journal of Education for Teaching*, 21(2): 191–217.

General Medical Council (GMC) (2004), *Guidance on Development Continuing Professional Development* at www.gmc-uk.org/education/pro_development/index.asp (accessed 16/01/06).

General Teaching Council for England (GTCE) (2004a) *Code of Conduct and Practice for Registered Teachers*. London and Birmingham: GTCE.

General Teaching Council for England (GTCE) (2004b) *The GTC Statement: The Statement of Professional Values and Practice for Teachers*, www.gtce.org.uk/standards/disc/StatementOfProf Values, accessed 10 October 2005.

General Teaching Council for Northern Ireland (GTCNI) (2004) *Code of Practice and Professional Standards*. Belfast: GTCNI.

General Teaching Council for Scotland (GTCS) (2002) *The Standard for Full Registration*. Edinburgh: GTCS.

General Teaching Council for Scotland (GTCS) (2003) *Achieving the Standard for Chartered Teacher Guidance for Teachers*. Edinburgh: GTCS.

General Teaching Council for Scotland (GTCS) (2003a) *Professional Code for Registered Teachers*. Edinburgh: GTCS.

General Teaching Council for Scotland (GTCS) (2003b) *Classroom Assistants: A GTC Scotland Position Paper May 2003*. Edinburgh: GTCS.

General Teaching Council for Scotland (GTCS) (2005) *Chartered Teachers Report from Questionnaire. Strategies for the Future and General Update*. Edinburgh: GTCS.

General Teaching Council for Wales (GTCW) (2002) *The Professional Code for Teachers*. Cardiff: GTCW.

Gilbert, T. (1995) nursing: empowerment and the problem of power, *Journal of Advanced Nursing*, 21: 865–71.

Gilbert, T. (2001) Reflective practice and clinical supervision: meticulous rituals of the confessional, *Journal of Advanced Nursing*, 36(2): 199–205.

Glaister, A. and Glaister, B. (2005) Space for growth, in A. Glaister and B. Glaister (eds), *Inter-Agency Collaboration – Providing for Children*. Edinburgh: Dunedin Academic Press. pp. 58–72.

Goddard, R. and O'Brien, P. (2003) Beginning teachers' perceptions of their work, well-being and intention to leave, *Asia-Pacific Journal of Teacher Education*, 6(2): 99–118.

Goleman, D. (1996) *Emotional Intelligence: Why It Can Matter More than IQ*. London: Bloomsbury.

Gould, B. and Masters, H. (2004) Learning to make sense: the use of critical incident analysis in facilitated reflective groups of mental health student nurses, *Learning in Health and Social Care*, 3: 53–63.

Grainger, T., Barnes, J. and Scoffham, S. (2004) A creative cocktail: creative teaching in initial teacher education, *Journal of Education for Teaching*, 30(3): 243–53.

Greenwood, J. (1993) Reflective practice: a critique of the work of Argyris and Schon. *Journal of Advanced Nursing*, 18: 1183–7.

Gregg, M. and Magilvy, J. (2001) Professional identity of Japanese nurses: bonding into nursing, *Journal of Health Sciences*, 3: 47–55.

Griffin, M.L. (2003) Using critical incidents to promote and assess reflective thinking in preservice teachers, *Reflective Practice*, 4(2): 207–20.

Habermas, J. (1987) *The Theory of Communicative Action*. Vol. 2, *Lifeworld and System: A Critique of Functional Reason*, trans. T. McCarthy. Boston, MA: Beacon Press.

Hall, C. (2004) Theorising changes in teachers' work, *Canadian Journal of Educational Administration and Policy*, 32. www.umanitoba.ca/publications/cjeap.

Hallam, S., Kirkton, A., Peffers, J., Robertson, P. and Stobart, G. (2004) *Evaluation of Project 1: Support for Professional Practice in Formative Assessment*. Final Report: Assessment is for Learning Development Programme. Edinburgh: Scottish Executive.

Handy, C. (1981) *Understanding Organizations*, 2nd edn. Harmondsworth: Penguin Books.

Hargreaves, A. (2000) Mixed emotions: teachers' perceptions of their interactions with students, *Teaching and Teacher Education*, 16(8): 811–26.

Harris, A. and Muijs, D. (2005) *Improving Schools Through Teacher Leadership*. Buckinghamshire: Open University Press.

Harrison, J.K., Lawson, T. and Wortley, A. (2005) Mentoring the beginning teacher: developing professional autonomy through critical reflection on practice, *Reflective Practice*, 6(3): 419–41.

Hascher, T., Cocard, Y. and Moser, P. (2004) Forget about theory – practice is all? Student teachers' learning in practicum, *Teachers and Teaching: Theory and Practice*, 10(6): 623–37.

Hastings, S. (2005) 'Advanced Skills Teachers' *Times Educational Supplement*, 4th March 2005. (last accessed 10/3/05) http://www.tes.co.uk/search/story/?story_id=2078814

Heath, H. (1998) Paradigm dialogues and dogma: finding a place for research, nursing models, and reflection, *Journal of Advanced Nursing*, 28(2): 288–94.

Helsby, G. (1996) Defining and developing professionalism in English secondary schools, *Journal of Education for Teaching*, 22(2): 135–48.

Her Majesty's Government (HMG) (2004) *Every Child Matters: Change for Children*. London: HM Government, from www.everychildmatters.gov.uk/_files/F9E3F941DC8D4580539EE4C743 E9371D.pdf, accessed 10 October 2005.

Her Majesty's Government (HMG) (2005) *Higher Standards: Better Schools for All: More Choice for Parents and Pupils*. White Paper. London: The Stationery Office.

Herzberg, F. (1968) *Work and the Nature of Man*. London: Staples Press.

House of Commons Education and Skills Committee (2004) *Secondary Education: Teacher Retention and Recruitment.* London: The Stationery Office, www.publications. parliament.uk/pa/cm200304/cmselect/cmeduski/1057/105703.htm(accessed 16/01/06).

Humes, W.M. (1986) *The Leadership Class in Scottish Education.* Edinburgh: John Donald.

Humphreys, M. and Hyland, T. (2002) Theory, practice and performance in teaching: professionalism, intuition and jazz, *Educational Studies,* 28(1): 5–15.

Husu, J. (2003) Real-world pedagogical ethics: mission impossible? *Teacher Development,* 7(2): 311–26.

Jensen, E. (1995) *The Learning Brain.* San Diego, CA: Turning Point.

Johansson, T. and Kroksmark, T. (2004) Teachers' intuition-in-action: how teachers experience action, *Reflective Practice,* 5(3): 357–81.

Johnson, H. and Castelli, M. (1999) The national professional qualification for head teachers: the need for additional support for candidates for Catholic leadership, *Journal of In-service Education,* 25(3): 519–32.

Johnson, M. and Hallgarten, J. (2002) The Future of the Teaching profession in M. Johnson and J. Hallgarten (eds) *From Victims of Change to Agents of Change: The Future of the Teaching Profession.* London: Institute for Public Policy Research.

Jones, P. (2004) 'They are not like us and neither should they be': issues of teacher identity for teachers of pupils with profound and multiple learning difficulties, *Disability and Society,* 19(2): 159–69.

Kassem, C.L. (2002) Developing the teaching professional: what teacher educators need to know about emotions, *Teacher Development,* 6(3): 363–73.

Kroger, J. (1986) *Identity in Adolescence: The Balance between Self and Other.* London and New York: Routledge.

Larrivee, B. (2000) Transforming teaching practice: becoming the critically reflective teacher, *Reflective Practice,* 1(3): 293–307.

Lave, J. and Wenger, E. (1991) *Situated Learning: Legitimate Peripheral Participation.* Cambridge: Cambridge University Press.

Lawton, D. (1992) *Education and Politics in the 1990s.* London: Falmer Press.

Mahony, P. and Hextall, I. (1998) *Transforming Professionalism: The TTA and the National Professional Qualifications in England and Wales.* TNTEE Publications Vol. 1 (2). London: Roehampton Institute.

Mahony, P., Menter, I. and Hextall, I. (2004) The emotional impact of Threshold Assessment on teachers in England, *British Education Research Journal,* 30(3).

Maich, N., Brown, B. and Royle, J. (2000) 'Becoming' through reflection and professional portfolios: the voice of growth in nurses, *Reflective Practice,* 1(3): 309–24.

Mamede, S. and Schmidt, H.G. (2004) The structure of reflective practice in medicine, *Medical Education,* 38(12): 1302–8.

Manuel, J. (2003). 'Such are the ambitions of youth': exploring issues of retention and attrition of early career teachers in New South Wales, *Asia-Pacific Journal of Teacher Education,* 31(2): 139–51.

Maslow, A. (1954) *Motivation and Personality.* New York: Harper.

Maynard, T. (2001) The students' teacher and the school community of practice: a consideration of 'learning as participation', *Cambridge Journal of Education*, 31(1): 39–52.

McCulloch, K., Tett, L. and Crowther, J. (2004) New community schools in Scotland: issues for inter-professional collaboration, *Scottish Educational Review*, 36(2): 129–44.

McLaughlin, T.H. (1999) Beyond the reflective teacher, *Educational Philosophy and Theory*, 31(1): 9–24.

McMahon, M. and Forde, C. (2005) Chartered teacher: enhancing teaching, enriching professionalism, *Professional Development Today*.

McNay, L. (1996) *Foucault: A Critical Introduction*. Cambridge: Polity Press.

McPhee, A., Forde, C. and Skelton, F. (2003) Teacher education in the UK in an era of performance management. *Asia Pacific Journal of Teacher Education and Development*, 6(2): 37–56.

McWilliam, E. (2000) The perfect corporate fit: new knowledge for new times, *International Journal of Leadership in Education*, 3(1): 75–83.

Menter, I., Holligan, C. and Mthenjwa, V. (2005) Reaching the parts that need to be reached? The impact of the Scottish Qualification for Headship, *School Leadership and Management*, 25(1): 7–23.

Menter, I., Mahony, P. and Hextall, I. (2004) Ne'er the twain shall meet? Modernizing the teaching profession in Scotland and England, *Journal of Education Policy*, 19(2): 195–214.

Menter, I., Mahony, P. and Hextall, I. (2006) What a performance! Impact of performance management and threshold assessment on the work and lives of primary teachers, in R.E. Webb (ed.), *Changing Teaching and Learning in the Primary Classroom*. Buckingham: Open University Press.

Menter, I., Muschamp, Y., Nicholls, P., Ozga, J. and Pollard, A. (1997) *Work and Identity in the Primary School – a Post-Fordist Analysis*. Buckingham: Open University Press.

Miehls, D. and Moffat, K. (2000) Constructing social work identity based on the reflective self, *British Journal of Social Work*, 30: 339–48.

Morris, E. (2001) Professionalism and trust – the future of teachers and teaching, speech to the Social Market Foundation, London, DfES.

Muijs, D. and Reynolds, D. (2003) The effectiveness of the use of learning support assistants in improving the mathematics achievement of low achieving pupils in primary school, *Educational Research*, 45(3): 19–30.

National Assembly of Wales (2001) *The Learning Country: A Paving Document. A Comprehensive Education and Lifelong Learning Programme to 2010 for Wales*. Cardiff: National Assembly for Wales.

National Remodelling Team (2003) Raising Standards and Tackling Workload: A National Agreement. London, DfES. http://www.remodelling.Org/what_na.php (last accessed 22/07/05).

Newell, R. (1992) Anxiety, accuracy and reflection: the limits of professional development, *Journal of Advanced Nursing*, 17: 1326–33.

Nias, J. (1989) *Primary Teachers Talking: A Study of Teaching as Work*. London: Routledge.

Nursing and Midwifery Council (NMC) (2004) *The NMC Code of Professional Conduct: Standards for Conduct, Performance and Ethics*.

Office for Standards in Education OFSTED, (2001), *Advanced Skills Teachers: Appointment, Deployment and Impact.* London: OFSTED.

Office for Standards in Education OFSTED (2003) *Advanced Skills Teachers – a Survey.* London: OFSTED.

Ohlen, J. and Segesten, K. (1998) The professional identity of the nurse: concept analysis and development, *Journal of Advanced Nursing,* 28(4): 720–27.

Office of Public Services Reform/(OPSR/DfES) (2002) *Schools Driving Forward Change* (interim report), www.cabinetoffice.gov.uk/opsr/local_service_projects/education/driving.asp, accessed 10 October 2005.

Organisation for Economic Co-operation and Development (OECD) (2001) *What Schools for the Future?* Paris: OECD.

Organisation for Economic Co-operation and Development (OECD) (2003) *Networks of Innovation: Towards New Models for Managing Schools and Systems.* Paris: OECD.

Organisation for Economic Co-operation and Development (OECD) (2005) *Teachers Matter: Attracting, Developing and Retaining Effective Teachers.* Paris: OECD.

Pask, E. (2003) Moral agency in nursing: seeing value in the work and believing that I make a difference, *Nursing Ethics,* 10(2): 165–74.

Paterson, L. (2003) *Scottish Education in the Twentieth Century.* Edinburgh: Edinburgh University Press

Pedro, J.Y. (2005) Reflection in teacher education: exploring pre-service teachers' meanings of reflective practice, *Reflective Practice,* 6(1): 49–66.

Phillips, D. and Ochs, K. (2003) Processes of policy borrowing in education: some analytical and explanatory devices, *Comparative Education,* 39 (4): 451–61.

Pickard, W., and Dobie, J. (2003) *The Political Context of Education after Devolution.* Edinburgh: Dunedin Academic Process.

Placier, M., Walker, M. and Foster, B. (2002) Writing the 'show-me' standards: teacher professionalism and political control in US state curriculum policy, *Curriculum Inquiry,* 32(2): 281–310.

Quality Assurance Agency for Higher Education (QAAHE) (2000) *The Standard for Initial Teacher Education in Scotland: Benchmark Information.* Gloucester: QUAAHE. October.

Randle, J. (2003) Changes in self-esteem during a 3 year pre-registration diploma in higher education (nursing) programme, *Learning in Health and Social Care,* 2(1): 51–60.

Rayner, S. and Gunter, H. (2005) Rethinking leadership: perspectives on remodelling practice, *Educational Review,* 57(2): 151–61.

Reeves, J. and l'Anson, J. (2005) Using CPD to assemble the means to act differently: constructing a personal 'war machine', Professional Enquiry in Education Seminar, University of Stirling, June 2, 2005.

Reeves, J. and Forde, C. (2004) The social dynamics of changing practice, *Cambridge Journal of Education,* 34(1): 85–102.

Reeves, J., Turner, E., Morris, B. and Forde, C. (2001) Exploring the impact of continuing professional development on practice in the context of the Scottish Qualification for Headship, *Journal of In-Service Education,* 27(2): 203–20.

Reeves, J., Turner, E., Morris, B. and Forde, C. (2005) Changing their minds: the social dynamics of school leaders' learning, *Cambridge Journal of Education*, 35(2): 255–73.

Reeves, J., Turner, E., Morris, B. and Forde, C. (2003) Culture and concepts of school leadership and management: exploring the impact of CPD on aspiring headteachers, *School Leadership & Management*, 23(1): 5–24.

Reicher, S. (2004) The context of social identity: domination, resistance and change, *Political Psychology*, 25(6): 921–45.

Reynolds, D., Muijs, D. and Treharne, D. (2003) Teacher evaluation and teacher effectiveness in the United Kingdom, *Journal of Personnel Evaluation in Education*, 17(1): 83–100.

Royal Pharmaceutical Society of Great Britain (2005), *Continuing Professional Development*, www.rpsgb.org.uk/members/cpd/index.htnl (26/10/05).

Rutter, M., Maugham, B., Mortimore, P. and Ouston, J. (1979) *Fifteen Thousand Hours*. London: Open Books.

Sachs, J. (2001) Teacher professional identity: competing discourses, competing outcomes, *Journal of Education Policy*, 16(2): 149–61.

Sachs, J. (2003) *The Activist Teaching Profession*. Buckingham: Open University Press.

Schein, E.H. (1980) *Organizational Psychology*, 3rd edn. Englewood Cliffs, NJ: Prentice-Hall.

Scott, C. and Dinham, S. (2002) The beatings will continue until quality improves: using carrots and sticks in the quest for educational improvement, *Teacher Development*, 6(1): 15–32.

Scottish Education Department (1965) *Primary Education in Scotland*. Edinburgh: HMSO.

Scottish Education Department/Consultative Committee on the Curriculum (SED/CCC) (1977) *The Structure of the Curriculum in the Third and Fourth Years of the Scottish Secondary School* (Munn Report). Edinburgh: HMSO.

Scottish Executive (2000) *Standards in Scotland's Schools etc Act*. Edinburgh: Scottish Executive.

Scottish Executive (2004a) *Ambitious, Excellent Schools: Our Agenda for Action*. Edinburgh: Scottish Executive.

Scottish Executive (2004b) *For Scotland's Children: Better Integrated children's services*. Edinburgh: Scottish Executive, www.scotland.gov.uk/library3/education/fcsr-00.asp, accessed 10 October 2005.

Scottish Executive (2005) Schools of Ambition, press release, February, www.scotland.gov.uk/ News/Releases/2005/02/23100017, accessed 29 September 2005.

Scottish Executive Education Department (SEED) (2001) *A Teaching Profession for the 21st Century. Agreement Reached Following Recommendations Made in the McCrone Report*. Edinburgh: SEED.

Scottish Executive Education Department (SEED) (2004) *Teachers in Scotland 2003*. Statistical Publication: Education Series. Edinburgh: Scottish Executive.

Scottish Executive Education Department (SEED) (2005) *The Impact of ICT Initiatives in Scottish Schools: Phase 3*. Edinburgh: SEED.

Scottish Office Education and Industry Department. (SOEID) (1998a) *A national frame-work for the continuing professional development of teachers.* Edinburgh: SOEID.

Scottish Office Education and Industry Department (SOEID) (1998b) *Proposals for Developing a Framework for the Continuing Professional Development of the Teaching Profession in Scotland.* Edinburgh: SOEID.

Sergiovanni, T. (1999) *The lifeworld of leadership: Creating culture, community, and personal meaning in our schools.* San Francisco: Jossey-Bass.

Sergiovanni, T. (2003) The lifeworld at the center: values and action in educational leadership, in N. Bennett, M. Crawford, and M. Cartwright (eds), *Effective Educational Leadership.* London: Paul Chapman Publishing.

Shapiro, J.P. and Stefkovich, J.A. (2001) *Ethical Leadership and Decision-making in Education.* Mahwah, NJ: Lawrence Erlbaum.

Shaughnessy, M.F. (2004) An interview with Anita Woolfolk: the educational psychology of teacher efficacy, *Educational Psychology Review*, 16(2): 153–76.

Simpson, M. (2005) *Assessment.* Edinburgh: Dunedin Academic Press.

Smithers, A. and Robinson, P. (2001) *Teachers leaving.* Centre for Education and Employment Research: University of Liverpool.

Soodak, L.C. and Podell, D.M. (1996) Teacher efficacy: towards the understanding of a multi-faceted construct, *Teaching & Teacher Education*, 12(4): 401–11.

Sparrow, J., Ashford, R. and Heel, D. (2005) A methodology to identify workplace features that can facilitate or impede reflective practice: a National Health Service UK study, *Reflective Practice*, 6(2): 189–97.

Spillane, J.P., Diamond, J.P., Sherer, J.Z. and Coldren, A.F. (2005) Distributing Leadership, in M. Coles and G. Southworth (eds), *Developing Leadership: creating schools for tomorrow.* Maidenhead: Open University Press.

Stokking, K., Leenders, F., de Jong, E. and van Tartwijk, J. (2003) From student to teacher: reducing practice shock and early dropout in the teaching profession, *European Journal of Teacher Education*, 26(3): 329–50.

Stoll, L. and Bolam, R. (2005) Developing leadership for learning communities, in M. Coles and G. Southworth (eds), *Developing Leadership: Creating Schools for Tomorrow.* Maidenhead: Open University Press.

Stoll, L. and Fink, D. (1996) *Changing Our Schools: Linking School Improvement and School Effectiveness.* Buckingham: Open University Press.

Stronach, I., Corbin, B., McNamara, O., Stark, S. and Warne, T. (2002) Towards an uncertain politics of professionalism: teacher and nurse identities in flux, *Journal of Education Policy*, 17(1): 109–38.

Sutherland, G. (2001) Examinations and the construction of professional identity: a case study of England 1800–1950, *Assessment in Education*, 8(1): 51–64.

Sutton, R.E. and Wheatley, K.F. (2003) Teachers' emotions and teaching: a review of the literature and directions for future research, *Educational Psychology Review*, 15(4): 327–58.

Taylor, C. (2003) Narrating practice: reflective accounts and the textual construction of reality, *Journal of Advanced Nursing*, 42(3): 244–51.

Taylor, C. and Jennings, S. (2004) *The Work of Advanced Skills Teachers*. Reading: Centre for British Teachers.

Teacher Training Agency (TTA) (2003) *Qualifying to Teach*. London: TTA.

Teachernet (2005a) *Chartered London Teacher*, www.teachernet.gov.uk/wholeschool/london/teachersandleaders/clt/ (accessed 27/10/05).

Teachernet (2005b) *Excellent Teacher Scheme (ETS) Explanatory Notes*, www.teachernet.gov.uk/ docbank/index.cfm?id=8482 (accessed 16/01/06).

Teachers' Agreement Communications Team (TACT) (2004) *School Leadership and Collegiality*, Scottish Executive and the Convention of Scottish Local Authorities, www.scottishcouncils.org/ tact, accessed 10 October 2005.

Thurlow Long, D. and Stuart, C. (2004) Supporting higher levels of reflection among teacher candidates: a pedagogical framework, *Teachers and Teaching: Theory and Practice*, 10(3): 275–90.

Times Educational Supplement (2003) Your Career – Career Moves – Advanced Skills Teachers.

Times Educational Supplement (TES) (2005a) Online Forum, 4 March, accessed 10 March 2005.

Times Educational Supplement (TES) (2005b) Online Forum 10 May, posting by Freddie92: TES Staff Room, accessed 29 October 2005.

Times Educational Supplement (2005c) Online Forum 28 March, accessed 29 October 2005.

Timperley, H. (2005) Distributed leadership: developing theory from practice, *Journal of Curriculum Studies*, 37(4): 395–420.

Tooley, J. (2000) *Reclaiming Education*. London: Cassell.

United Nations Commission on Human Rights (UNCHR) (1991) *Convention on the Rights of the Child*. New York: United Nations Department of Public Information.

US Department of Education (USDofE) (2001) No child left behind, www.ed.gov/policy/elsec/leg/ esea02/index.html, accessed 12 July 2005.

Volkmann, M. and Anderson, M. (1998) Creating professional identity; dilemmas and metaphors of a first-year chemistry teacher, *Science Education*, 82: 293–310.

Warnock, M. (2005) *Special Educational Needs: A New Look*. Impact No. 11. London: Philosophy of Education Society of Great Britain.

Webb, P.T. (2005) The anatomy of accountability, *Journal of Education Policy*, 20(2): 189–208.

Webb, R., Vulliamy, G., Hamalainen, S., Sarja, A., Kimonen, E. and Nevalainen, R. (2004) A comparative analysis of primary teacher professionalism in England and Finland, *Comparative Education*, 40 (1): 84–107.

Wedge, P. and Prosser, H. (1973) *Born to Fail: The National Children's Bureau on the Striking Differences in the Lives of British Children*. London: Arrow Books.

Weick, K.E. (1995) *Sense Making in Organizations*. Thousand Oaks, CA: Sage Publications.

Weiss, E.M. (1999) Perceived workplace conditions and first-year teachers' morale, career choice commitment, and planned retention: a secondary analysis – when teaching is more than a job, *Teaching and Teacher Education*, 15(8): 861–79.

Wenger, E. (1998) *Communities of Practice: Learning, Meaning and Identity*. Cambridge: Cambridge University Press.

Wilson, V., Schlapp, U. and Davidson, J. (2003) An 'extra pair of hands'? Managing classroom assistants in Scottish primary schools, *Educational Management and Administration*, 31(2): 189–204.

Wintour, P. and Bates, S. (1993) Major goes back to the old values, *Guardian*, http://politics.guardian. co.uk/politicspast/story/0,9061,801926,00.html, accessed 18 July 2005.

Woodhead, C. (2002) *Class War*. London: Little, Brown.

Woods, M. (2005) Nursing ethics education: are we really delivering the good(s)? *Nursing Ethics*, 12(1): 5–18.

Woods, P. and Jeffrey, B. (2002) The reconstruction of primary teachers' identities, *British Journal of Sociology of Education*, 23(1): 89–106.

Woolfson, R. and Truswell, E. (2005) Do classroom assistants work? *Educational Research*, 47(1): 63–75.

Wright, N. and Bottery, M. (1997) Perceptions of professionalism by the mentors of student teachers, *Journal of Education for Teaching*, 23(3): 235–52.

Index

Added to a page number 'f' denotes a figure and 'n' denotes notes.